JUST A LITTLE WALK WITH JESUS
A LENTEN SPIRITUAL SAUNTER WITH JESUS

Bruce G. Epperly

Energion Publications
Cantonment, Florida
2025

Copyright © 2025, Bruce G. Epperly. All rights reserved.

Scripture quotations are taken from the New Revised Standard Version Updated Edition. Copyright © 2021 National Council of Churches of Christ in the United States of America. Used by permission. All rights reserved worldwide.

Cover Design: Henry Neufeld
Cover Image: Adobe Stock

ISBN: 978-1-63199-964-2
eISBN: 978-1-63199-965-9

Energion Publications
1241 Conference Rd
Cantonment, FL 32533

pubs@energion.com

Contents

1. A Spiritual Saunter with Mark's Gospel 1
2. Mark's Saunter with Jesus 9
3. Sauntering with Jesus and Mark 13
4. A Spiritual Saunter with Jesus 17

Day 1	Preparing for the Journey	19
Day 2	You are God's Beloved Child	21
Day 3	Wisdom in the Wilderness	23
Day 4	Now is the Day of Salvation	25
Day 5	Living in the Immediate	27
Day 6	Liberating Spirit	29
Day 7	Healed for Service	31
Day 8	Morning Prayer	33
Day 9	God Wants to Heal You	35
Day 10	The Faith of Friends Can Heal the World	37
Day 11	A World without Outsiders	40
Day 12	Stretch Out Your Hand	42
Day 13	A Harvest of Righteousness	44
Day 14	Small is Bountiful	46
Day 15	Peace in the Storm	48
Day 16	Peace for the Troubled Soul	50
Day 17	The Energy of Love	53
Day 18	Give Her Something to Eat	55
Day 19	When God Can't	57
Day 20	A Center in the Cyclone	59
Day 21	A Social Safety Net	61
Day 22	Meditation and Movement	63
Day 23	The Fringe of Jesus' Coat	65
Day 24	Ever-Expanding Grace	67
Day 25	Taking Your Medicine in a Prayerful Way	69

Day 26	Corporate Compassion	71
Day 27	Gradual Healing	73
Day 28	Who is Jesus?	75
Day 29	God Feels Our Pain	78
Day 30	On the Mountaintop	80
Day 31	In the Valley of Chaos, God is With Us	82
Day 32	Greatness in Service	84
Day 33	Many Paths, Many Healers	86
Day 34	Blessing the Children	88
Day 35	Wealth that Lasts	90
Day 36	The Way of the Cross	92
Day 37	Glory that Matters	94
Day 38	What Do You Want God to Do for You?	96
Day 39	The Tale of Two Parades	97
Day 40	Who Will Roll Away the Stone for Us?	99
Day 41	An Empty Tomb and an Open Future	101

CHAPTER ONE
A SPIRITUAL SAUNTER WITH MARK'S GOSPEL

> I want Jesus to walk with me.
> I want Jesus to walk with me.
> All along my pilgrim journey,
>
> Lord, I want Jesus to walk with me.[1]

I invite you to join me and the author of Mark's Gospel on a forty-one-day holy adventure whose impact will last a lifetime. Mark's gospel proclaims the good news of movement and the lively presence of God's revelation on the crowded paths of life. In the first ten chapters of Mark, Jesus is constantly on the move. Looking toward the horizons of Jerusalem as the fulfillment of his vocation, Jesus is continually on the road. His home is on the highways and byways, the mountain tops and the seashore. Accompanied by his closest followers, Jesus engages in a pilgrimage of healing, wholeness, and prophetic ministry. Each day is an adventure as Jesus encounters fellow pilgrims on the walk of life: a synagogue leader desperately seeking a healing for his daughter, an outcast woman with a flow of blood, a sight impaired man crying out for a cure, a helpless man possessed by a demon, a hardworking group of fishermen on the Sea of Galilee. Each day is a surprise. Random encounters lead to transformed lives. Movement leads to mission and mission moves body, mind, spirit, and relationships. Jesus has a vision of the far horizon, but he does not have an agenda. He leaves the working out of his vision to apparently random, but truly providential encounters, he has along

---
1 "I Want Jesus to Walk with Me," African American Spiritual.

the way. Each moment is a thin place, a meeting place, of the Infinite and the intimate, the holy and the hurt.

The watch word for Mark's gospel is "immediately" just as "rejoice" is the affirmation of Philippian spirituality and "unfettered" describes the expanding circle of the Christian movement portrayed in the Acts of the Apostles. Jesus encounters a person in need of transformation and immediately springs into action, either by word, touch, or movement. When his healing work is done, Jesus is back on the road, energized by a vision but open to surprise. Deeply centered in prayer, Jesus' rootedness is the springboard for action. Jesus not only speaks the good news of God's realm, but Jesus is also the incarnation of God's good news in action. Moments of quiet contemplation lead to compassionate activism to embody God's realm on earth as it is in heaven.

We can imagine Jesus walking down the streets of our neighborhood, whether it is urban, small town, or rural, looking deeply into the spirits of everyone who passes by. We can visualize him walking by our home, library, shopping center, place of business, or favorite haunt and engaging us in conversation, and then surprising us with the invitation, "Follow me," presenting us with the choice to stand still in comfortable and safe familiarity or move forward on a holy adventure with Jesus as our companion. If we are troubled in body, mind, spirit, or relationships, Jesus might speak a word of affirmation, pray with us, and touch us on the forehead. He might even give us financial or political advice as we plan for our own or our nation's future. As Biblical scholar, physician, and organist Albert Schweitzer asserts in the final words of his epoch-making *Quest for the Historical Jesus*, we will find God in the movement and in moving with the Savior, we will discover not only who Jesus is but who we really are as we discover our vocations for just such a time as this.

> He comes to us as One unknown, without a name, as of old, by the lakeside, He came to those men who knew Him not. He speaks to us the same words: "Follow thou me!" and sets us to the

tasks which He has to fulfill for our time. He commands. And to those who obey Him, whether they be wise or simple, He will reveal himself in the toils, the conflicts, the sufferings which they shall pass through in His fellowship, and, as an ineffable mystery, they shall learn in their own experience Who He is.

Mark is inviting us to know Jesus in the movements of life: in God's presence in the challenges of our time, and in our own daily responsibilities. God's realm has drawn near to us not just in the first century but in the maelstrom of the twenty-first century in which self-proclaimed Christians have turned from the power of love to the love of power and Caesar has eclipsed Jesus as their moral compass.

Jesus moved as a free person despite living as a Jew, without political power or personal rights, in an occupied land. From a political point of view, Jesus never spent one moment of his life as a free self-determining person. Yet, his spirit soared, untrammeled by Roman oppression or the confining rules of his religious tradition. As long as your spirit can move, you are free. As long as you choose to follow God's way, no prison can confine you. Even stuck in prison, like Paul and Silas, you will discover that if you have a song in your heart, your spirit moves and the prison bars open.

I began writing this Lenten journey on July 17, 2025, the day of political and civil rights leader John Lewis' birthday. As many of us pondered our spiritual responsibilities in this troubled time in the United States, I chanced to come upon words from one of John Lewis' last interviews, shortly before his death from pancreatic cancer. When reporter Jonathan Capehart asked him "what he would say to people who feel as though they have already been giving it their all but nothing seems to change," Lewis answered: "You must be able and prepared to give until you cannot give any more. We must use our time and our space on this little planet that we call Earth to make a lasting contribution, to leave it a little better than we found it, and now that need is greater than ever before." A year before his death,

Lewis uttered these immortal lines, providing an interpretation of the way of Jesus in these troubled times.

> Do not get lost in a sea of despair Do not become bitter or hostile. Be hopeful, be optimistic. Never, ever be afraid to make some noise and get in good trouble, necessary trouble. We will find a way to make a way out of no way.

During Lent, we discover that God is with us, making a way where we see no way forward. We wander the forty-year pathway toward freedom with the children of Israel, no longer slaves in Egypt, and yearning for a promised land. We face our own forty days of reflection and temptation with Jesus, seeking spiritual guidance for our use of our power and privilege and finding ways to resist temptation and tyranny with courage and compassion. We come with burdens and brokenness to receive God's blessing and receive Jesus' healing touch. We discover that in the wilderness we are not alone. Jesus is walking right beside us. Bidden or unbidden, to paraphrase Carl Jung, Jesus is our companion, and we will know him in the journey.

I am inviting you on a spiritual saunter during the Lenten season. Sauntering is identified with walking at a leisurely pace, taking in the wonders and beauties of life. A sauntering spirit pauses and notices and lets their experience of beauty and surprise guide their steps. To saunter in the spirit is to be a person whose doors of perception have been opened, as William Blake notes, to see the world as it really is – Infinite! In his essay "Walking," North American mystic Henry David Thoreau gave what is perhaps the most insightful description of sauntering:

> I have met with but one or two persons in the course of my life who understood the art of Walking, that is, of taking walks — who had a genius, so to speak, for *sauntering*, which word is beautifully derived from idle people who roved about the country, in the Middle Ages, and asked charity, under pretense of going *a la Sainte Terre,* to the Holy Land, till the children exclaimed,

"There goes a Sainte-Terrer," a Saunterer, a Holy-Lander. They who never go to the Holy Land in their walks, as they pretend, are indeed mere idlers and vagabonds; but they who do go there are saunterers in the good sense, such as I mean.

The Concord mystic, whose mystic vision led him to oppose the Mexican-American War (1846-1848), work for the abolition of slavery, and provide comfort for pilgrims traveling the Underground Railroad continues.

Some, however, would derive the word from *sans terre*, without land or a home, which, therefore, in the good sense, will mean, having no particular home, but equally at home everywhere. For this is the secret of successful sauntering. He who sits still in a house all the time may be the greatest vagrant of all; but the saunterer, in the good sense, is no more vagrant than the meandering river, which is all the while sedulously seeking the shortest course to the sea.

You can saunter over countrysides and beaches with Thoreau, wander with an open-spirited sense of purpose on your predawn walk as I daily join prayer and exercise in the woods of the Washington DC suburb of Potomac, Maryland, or claim the title of *flaneur* or *flaneuse* who strolls through urban spaces, stopping occasionally for a snack or coffee, to experience the many sights of the city, motivated by a sense of spiritual and intellectual curiosity. Each person you meet is an angel in disguise, a revelation of the Holy, despite their often troubling and fearful disguises. You can imagine Jesus walking beside you or train your eyes for burning bushes hidden around every corner. In sauntering, you may hear bird songs for the first time, and receive divine revelations, as I occasionally do, hidden in the melodies of black birds, sparrows, blue jays, and crows. God speaks to us everywhere and with every footstep we are walking on holy ground as saunterers and flaneurs and flaneuses of the Spirit. When you walk with Jesus, you are always at home, even if the way forward is uncertain.

Lent is a time of self-examination. An opportunity to look at our lives honesty and openly, knowing that God is out to heal us, not to harm us. During Lent, Jesus walks beside us. In moving with Jesus as our companion, we move our spirits as well as our bodies and the circumference of our compassion expands to embrace all creation. Like the first century companions of Jesus, both women and men, following Jesus challenges us to look toward the horizons of God's spiritual and moral arcs, aiming at justice and compassion. In walking with Jesus, each day becomes a holy adventure, filled with wonder and surprise, and challenge and creativity.

In our Lenten sauntering, our steps begin to align with Jesus' steps as a companion we imitate not a judge we fear. Even if our condition limits our movements, we can still visualize Jesus right beside us, sharing his vision and inviting us to embody his love in our own unique way. The walking Jesus wants us to fulfill our vocation in our own unique way. Jesus invites us to be agents of our adventures in companionship with the Great Adventurer who walks beside us every step of the way. In the spirit of the poem, "Footprints," Jesus quietly and anonymously carries us during those times when we can no longer walk ourselves. And when we find ourselves at the place we call home, we will marvel, "Over and over, over and over, my soul looks back and wonders how I got over."[2]

Let us saunter with Jesus during Lent, open to unexpected providence and new horizons of faith. God has given us a spiritual GPS and God has also given us the invitation to change course and take new routes with Jesus beside us. The adventure begins. Let prayer and song be our guide on this pilgrim journey with Jesus.

I want Jesus to walk with me.

> I want Jesus to walk with me.
> All along my pilgrim journey,
> Lord, I want Jesus to walk with me.

---

2   "How I Got Over," Clara Ward.

In my trials, Lord, walk with me.
In my trials, Lord, walk with me.
When my heart is almost breaking,
Lord, I want Jesus to walk with me.

When I'm troubled, Lord, walk with me.
When I'm troubled, Lord, walk with me.
When my head is bowed in sorrow,
Lord, I want Jesus to walk with me.[3]

---

[3] "I Want Jesus to Walk with Me," African American Spiritual.

CHAPTER TWO
MARK'S SAUNTER WITH JESUS

> Guide my feet while I run this race,
> Guide my feet while I run this race,
> Guide my feet while I run this race,
> for I don't want to run this race in vain![4]

Mark takes us on a saunter with Jesus. Today, he might have gone on a road trip but long ago and faraway walking was the primary mode of transportation for working people and the peasant class. The first ten chapters of Mark's Gospel describe Jesus' pilgrimage through Judea leading up to Jesus' final days in Jerusalem. For Mark, Jesus' destination is Jerusalemand the Cross, the Empy Tomb and the Open Future, but on the way the Healer and his companions have many unexpected adventures, and on the journey, they discover who Jesus' identity and their own vocations.

Mark's Gospel is a combination of imagination and recollection. Not his own personal and first-hand recollections, but likely those of Peter, and Peter's associates, according to the accounts of early church theologians, including Bishop Papias (60-130 CE) and Bishop Irenaeus (125-202 CE) who claim that John Mark wrote his gospel based on Peter's sermons. It is likely the Gospel of Mark was written between 65 and 75 CE and that the author never personally met Jesus. Mark is a collector of stories whose aim is to present the good news of Jesus the Healer and Savior for generations to come. Although he talks about the return of the Messiah, Mark doesn't have a Second Com-

---

4   "Guide My Feet," African American Spiritual.

ing calendar. He's far more interested in the Millisecond Coming, the moment-by-moment healing presence of Jesus in the lives of his disciples and in our daily lives. Yet, in listening to the stories of Jesus, the author of Mark was transformed and found his voice, and as the hymn says, he loved to tell the story!

The identity of the author of Mark's Gospel will likely remain unknown. Still, the author was a person of faithful imagination and literary skill as well as heartfelt emotion. This is holistic theology and spirituality at its best. Truly inspired by the Jesus he followed, there is not a throwaway word in Mark's Gospel. He chooses his words carefully with only one aim in mind: to share the good news of Jesus whose life and message transforms and gives purpose to peoples' lives.

As the earliest written gospel, Mark's biography of Jesus details only a fraction of Jesus' life. The author of John's Gospel rightly notes that "Jesus did many other things as well. If every one of them were written down, I suppose that even the whole world would not have room for the books that would be written." (John 21:25) Among the many stories Mark heard from Peter and Jesus' intimate female and male followers, Mark selected those which best illuminated Jesus' ministry of healing and wholeness, Jesus' vocation as God's Messiah and Chosen Messenger, and Jesus' willingness to sacrifice his life for our salvation. Jesus the Healer and Savior is always more than we can imagine and can never be encompassed by doctrine, dogma, or description. That's good news. In the spirit of Augustine, if we think we can fully know Jesus, we have created a Jesus of our own making and not the Healer of Galilee, whose power and love still shape us today.

Why did Mark write the Gospel? Mark was inspired to put the stories of Jesus on papyrus, choosing some and omitting others, like a novelist or preacher. While we can't fully intuit Mark's motivations, let me suggest a few possibilities.

Mark experienced the power of Jesus to heal our cells and souls and wanted to share that power with the world.

Mark believed that a historical record of Jesus' life needed to be preserved for future generations. While Mark made no claim to know the future, he believed that the future was in God's hands, whether this future involves ten or ten thousand years. "But about that day or hour no one knows, neither the angels in heaven nor the Son, but only the Father." (Mark 13:32) In the meantime, we need to tell the stories of Jesus that heal and empower and deliver us from the fear of sin and death.

Mark imagined that in future generations people like us would be reading the stories of Jesus. While Mark could not visualize our age of communications and travel, social media and interstellar voyages, he wrote for the ages as well as from the perspective of his concrete moment in history. The Gospel is always concrete and timely even when it speaks of God's infinity. The "old, old story," the story of the Love that created the universe and the stars, is as current as today's news feed and the stories of Jesus' healing power are as real today as they were two thousand years ago as he walked the paths of Judea.

Mark believes words transform lives. The word is made flesh in Mark's Jesus, and we can imagine Jesus walking alongside us as we read Mark's Gospel. Jesus is our companion, and we can count on his healing wisdom in every season of life.

Written in an earlier era to edify the earliest Christian communities, Mark still speaks to us and invites to get up "immediately" in response to Jesus' call. In walking with Jesus, we will discover who we are, who he is, and whose we are.

> Hold my hand while I run this race,
> Hold my hand while I run this race,
> Hold my hand while I run this race,
> for I don't want to run this race in vain!
>
> I'm Your child while I run this race,
> I'm Your child while I run this race,
> I'm Your child while I run this race,
> for I don't want to run this race in vain!

Search my heart while I run this race,
Search my heart while I run this race,
Search my heart while I run this race,
for I don't want to run this race in vain!
Guide my feet while I run this race,
Guide my feet while I run this race,
Guide my feet while I run this race,
for I don't want to run this race in vain!

CHAPTER THREE
SAUNTERING WITH JESUS AND MARK

> O Master, let me walk with thee
> In lowly paths of service free;
> Tell me thy secret; help me bear
> The strain of toil, the fret of care.[5]

This book was born on a walk. In the predawn hours of a July 2025 morning as I was meditating on the words of John Lewis, I set out on my walk through the wooded neighborhoods of Potomac, Maryland, the Washington DC suburb I call home. I had been reading Mark's Gospel for the past month, to deepen my encounter with the Living Jesus and incubating ideas for a possible devotional book, but not sure that I was the one to write it. Earlier, after my morning meditation, I foolishly – or providentially – glanced at my newsfeed and was overwhelmed by worry at the state of our nation and the planet. In a matter of moments, I was confronted by extreme weather patterns and forest fires symptomatic of global climate change; the continuing atrocities in Ukraine and Gaza; the targeted attack on brown skinned undocumented residents by masked ICE agents; and attacks on democracy and civil rights by political leaders. I also chanced – or was it providence? – to see a quote from John Lewis, urging me to keep the faith in troubled times. While I did not give in to the chaos portrayed by my newsfeed, I needed spiritual support to maintain hope and work to further God's vision of Shalom. As I walked through the woods across from our townhouse neighborhood,

---

5   "O Master, Let Me Walk with Thee," George Washington Gladden.

I felt Jesus walking beside me, urging me to look toward the horizons of hope and do what is in my power to share his gospel of love, justice, and hospitality. In companionship with Jesus, I discerned that there was a multitude of saunterers, good ancestors who kept their eyes on the prize and walked through the storm with hope in their hearts and hospitality in their hands – John Lewis, Howard Thurman, Teilhard de Chardin, Alfred North Whitehead, Fannie Lou Hamer, Francis of Assisi, Dorothy Day, Madaleine L'Engle, Peace Pilgrim, Oscar Romero, and the faithful pilgrims who've inspired my own journey of life. In the quiet moments of the morning, writing this book became my calling, and over the ensuing weeks, the words flowed in and through me, with a call and response from God, the author of Mark's Gospel, my good ancestors, and my own prayerful agency.

As a teacher, preacher, and writer, I felt the urge to do share my gifts to my fellow pilgrims, people like you, weary from the daily erosion of decency and democracy in our nation. Walking along I was drawn to Mark's Gospel, my favorite of the four canonical gospels, as a source of wisdom and courage for just such a time as now. I heard a whisper, "Walk with Mark's Gospel. Take Jesus on a walk as you read the Gospel. Invite others to talk a little walk with Jesus."

In the weeks that followed the inspiration to write this text, I returned to my previous meditations on Mark's Gospel, read a passage from Mark, focusing on those that describe Jesus on the move, as I took my morning walk, letting words and images come to me and then writing them down when I returned home. Although I walk at a three mile an hour clip, the images that came to me were that of a "saunter," to use the language of Henry David Thoreau. To walk forward joining purpose with aimlessness and intentionality with serendipity and synchronicity. In the interplay of divine inspiration and my theological and spiritual agency, words and images flowed into text you are reading today. I penned the final words of the pre-edited version of this text on August 6, 2025, another milestone date in human history, the eightieth anniversary of the dropping of the nuclear bomb on Hiroshima. As we face challenges that often dwarf our abilities, we need Jesus to walk with us, and in our walking we will discover our calling for just such a time as now.

On the trail and pavement, I experienced Jesus walking beside me, and like the characters of Mark's Gospel, the two of us engaged in a dynamic and evolving conversation. I want to walk with Jesus, and I want to gain his wisdom and compassion for this troubled time. I want to learn from Jesus and apply what I have learned as an agent of God's Realm in my family, friendships, congregational leadership, teaching, writing, and citizenship. I want to keep walking with Jesus, and I pray that Jesus walks with me in the coming seasons of life and receives me lovingly at the moment of death and beyond. Perhaps, you will want to walk with Jesus as well and experience him as your companion, guide, and challenger.

Revelations on the Walk with Jesus. I believe that God's revelations and insights touch everyone for theologians and pastors to children and politicians. God speaks to us in sound and silence, in meditation and movement, and prayer and protest, and God is moving in your life guiding you, mostly anonymously, toward your own holy land. Without getting into the intricacies of Christology, I believe Jesus is the Christ, the incarnate presence of God, and that the universal Christ, the Logos of John and the Sophia of the Wisdom, are one and the same in spirit. And, Jesus, the fully human is also the living presence of God's Creative and Loving Wisdom, not limited by time or space. The Infinite Wisdom of God takes birth in our finite lives as it did in humble Bethlehem. Wherever we are, God with us, Christ is with us, Spirit is with us, and Jesus is with us.

As you read this text, my prayer is that Jesus will come alive as your companion on the walk of life and that God's Loving Wisdom will inspire, illumine, and empower you for just such a time as now. I pray that this text will give you guidance for your path. Let us walk together hand in hand as companions with the sauntering Jesus.

> O Master, let me walk with thee
> In lowly paths of service free;

Tell me thy secret; help me bear
The strain of toil, the fret of care.

Help me the slow of heart to move
By some clear, winning word of love;
Teach me the wayward feet to stay,
And guide them in the homeward way.

Teach me thy patience; still with thee
In closer, dearer company,
In work that keeps faith sweet and strong,
In trust that triumphs over wrong.

In hope that sends a shining ray
Far down the future's broadening way;
In peace that only thou canst give,
With thee, O Master, let me live. (George Washington Gladden)

CHAPTER FOUR
A SPIRITUAL SAUNTER WITH JESUS

> Just a closer walk with Thee
> Grant it Jesus, is my plea
> Daily walking close to Thee
> Let it be, dear Lord, let it be.[6]

While this text was initially aimed for the season of Lent, it is relevant to any season of life. Its forty-one days are no accident. The extra day of this saunter with Jesus points to the Empty Tomb and the Open Future of Mark's resurrection story. The story of Jesus is never ending and each generation and each person encounters their own vision of Jesus, fitted to their life and the calling to be God's companion in healing their lives and this Good Earth.

There is no hurry when you saunter, so go at the pace that is right for you in body, mind, and spirit. You can do a meditation each day or ruminate for several days on each meditation. God has sown the seeds of wholeness in your life and is nurturing them to fullness with you. Even if you are not ambulatory, you can take a journey without distance. Jesus not only walks with us, but Jesus also sits beside us, providing companionship and challenge for our current situation.

There are many ways to saunter with Jesus. Indeed, Jesus comes to us in the way we need and when we need it, and inspires us to the spiritual path right for this unique season of life. The saying, "Pray as you can, not as you can't," applies to this text. One way I have found helpful is the following:

---

6 "Just a Closer Walk with Thee," anonymous.

Begin with a few minutes of stillness.

Ask Jesus to be your companion throughout the day.

Read the daily scripture and devotional reading.

Take the insights of each devotional reading out for a walk, letting the words inspire you as you connect them to your life.

Upon returning home, you may choose to write down your insights in a journal, or an affirmation that describes your experience.

Throughout the day, pause to remember the theme of the day and its relevance to your life.

Another meaningful Lenten sauntering practice that may be helpful in your sauntering with this text is a variation on what author Madeleine L'Engle describes as "kything." From the ancient Scottish, "to make known," kything is an act of spiritual or emotional connection in which we join with another in spirit. For example, you can invite Jesus to walk beside you, visualizing Jesus in a way that speaks to your spirit, and then simply let Jesus walk beside you, sharing his wisdom and love. Jesus is the Great Ancestor who constantly walks beside us. Yet like the person described in the poem, "Footprints," we are unaware of Jesus' presence beside us as a fellow pilgrim, who carries us when we've lost our way. In kything, we simply choose to be aware Jesus' presence as our intimate companion in our spiritual practices and throughout the day. The Jesus Movement is on the move and is growing in your life with every step you take! God is here, and God is near.

Go in peace! Keep a song in your heart to match the rhythm of your footsteps. God's truth is marching on! God is with you as you saunter with Jesus!

> I am weak but Thou art strong;
> Jesus, keep me from all wrong;
> I'll be satisfied as long
> As I walk, let me walk close to Thee.

Day One
Preparing for the Journey

> *See, I am sending my messenger ahead of you,*
> *who will prepare your way,*
> *the voice of one crying out in the wilderness:*
> *"Prepare the way of the Lord;*
> *make his paths straight."* (Mark 1:2-3)

Take time to read meditatively Mark 1:1-8 and then take the long-haired counter-culture preacher John the Baptist on a walk with you. Every adventure requires preparation, and spiritual adventures are no exception. As you take your first steps this morning, let go of the past and begin afresh. God is faithful, and God's mercies are new every morning, inviting us to be, as Thomas Celeno describes Francis of Assisi, "always fresh, always new, always beginning again."

John the Baptist is the ultimate outsider and counter cultural crusader. He looks as if he comes straight out of Golden Gate Park or Big Sur in the 1960's, two meccas of my youthful adventures, challenging the status quo and presenting in prophetic fashion an alternative vision of reality and new way of life. To make John the Baptist come alive, you might view John the Baptist singing "Prepare ye the way of the Lord," and the wondrous chaos that ensues in the opening segments of the musical "Godspell."

For those who repent and turn their lives around, choosing to follow a different path in their spiritual lives, the promise is forgiveness. The promise is a fresh start, with new values and commitments. The issue is not some everlasting heaven or hell, but our spiritual state in this lifetime: who will we follow, God or Caesar? Self-interest or world loyalty? Integrity or dishonesty?

We can see the horizon of God's realm coming to us, but we need to prepare our hearts for God's new birth in our lives.

This morning, invite John the Baptist to saunter in the wilderness with you. In our time of political turmoil and uncertainty, like the first century, ask John to open your eyes to your complicity with the evils of our time. Ask John how you might experience the baptism of God's Spirit in your life today and as you plan for the future. What will turning around and finding a new route mean for you in this troubled time?

With John as your companion, open your senses to God's call in your newsfeed, in the flora and fauna around you, in changing weather patterns, in the faces of your closest human and non-human companions. In the spirit of "Godspell," you might dance and sing in celebration of God's present Shalom, the Realm of Justice, Peace, and Healing, that will outlast all the prevaricators, power mongers, and potentates.

Breathe deeply the Breath of Freedom and Creativity as you prepare to embrace the horizons of God's future for you and the world.

Awaken me, Sauntering Companion, to wonder and beauty all around me. Challenge my assumptions and limitations. Give me insight and courage to embrace the Good News of Jesus in this troubled time and become a witness to the power of love to transform the world. In Jesus' Name. Amen.

Day Two
You are God's Beloved Child

> *Jesus saw the heavens torn apart and the Spirit descending like a dove upon him. And a voice came from the heavens, "You are my Son, the Beloved; with you I am well pleased."* (Mark 1:10-11)

As you read Mark 1:9-11, take the path to the Jordan River with all its beauty and turmoil. Jesus never experienced a moment of freedom, living in territory occupied by Rome. Today, the Palestinian citizens of the West Bank and Gaza similarly experience occupation, violence, and hopelessness. Like Judeans of Jesus' day, they live in hope of freedom and self-determination. Jesus comes into a world like ours – a world of tragic beauty, of love and hate, of hope and conflict – and experiences God's call to heal the Earth. His spirit soars to the heavens and returns to Earth with God's healing power.

There are unique moments in our lives when God becomes real to us, the heavens are opened, and we claim our vocation. Jesus heard God's blessing and felt divine energy and inspiration flow through him. "You are my Son, the Beloved; with you I am well pleased."

God speaks these same words to you and offers the Spirit of loving power and compassionate creativity. "You are my beloved child, and you are loved." This is God's original blessing that comes to us with each new morning. As the Celtic saint Pelagius affirms, in the visage of every newborn we can see God's face. To those who clung to original sin, this affirmation was an anathema and led to Pelagius' excommunication. But Pelagius was right! You are God's child. You are loved. You matter. You can do something wonderful with your life. As theologian Henri Nouwen affirms, "We are beloved, broken, and blessed." Even in our brokenness, God is blessing us, reminding us always that we are God's beloved children – and there's nothing we can do about it!

This morning, step forward with the affirmation, "I am God's beloved child. I am loved." Let those words resonate with every step, casting out the darkness of low self-esteem and passivity. "I am God's child, and I can do something beautiful for God," as Mother (Saint) Teresa counsels. When you return home from your sauntering, as you wash your face and hands or take a shower or bath, feel God's cleansing love bathing you in new life and filling you with the energy of healing and creativity. God's Spirit rests upon you and inspires you to claim your role as God's beloved and committed companion in healing the world.

Take me, O God of New Life, to the River Jordan. Cleanse me of yesterday's pain and brokenness. Refresh and restore me to be your companion in bringing beauty to this Good Earth and all its peoples. In Jesus' Name. Amen.

Day Three
Wisdom in the Wilderness

> *And the Spirit immediately drove Jesus out into the wilderness. He was in the wilderness forty days, tested by Satan, and he was with the wild beasts, and the angels waited on him.* (Mark 1:12-13)

As you reflect on Mark 1:12-13, ponder the tests you face in your saunter with Jesus. Often our greatest gifts and temptations are linked. For many of us, the storms of life are quiet and unobservable to our closest companions. Yet, the quiet storm, the inner temptation, hidden from the world is often a greater challenge than the maelstroms of relationships and citizenship that buffet us in this troubled time.

The Spirit immediately drives Jesus into the wilderness. Jesus has received great spiritual power that can be used for good or ill. His ability to serve as the embodiment of God's way is dependent on his self-awareness and purity of heart. As a Spirit Person, Jesus must commit to using his spiritual and relational power for good. He must put world loyalty ahead of self-interest and self-aggrandizement.

In a culture that glorifies power, success, individualism, and greed and sees social well-being and commitment to the common good as subservient to self-interest, Jesus' path is always countercultural. Yet, for Jesus' companions on the Way, letting go of self-interest is the pathway to abundant life.

Jesus sojourns with wild beasts. Wild beasts are also God's children and can be our spiritual companions. Wild beasts can also threaten our safety. Still, when we journey "where the wild things are," we are not alone. Angels watch over us. Divine messengers constantly provide inspiration and guidance with each step we take and protect us from sins of our own doing as well as the powers of evil that threaten our well-being.

With God as our companion, we are never alone and without resources. As you travel forth on life's pathway, remember God's angels accompany every step.

Guide my path, Fellow Pilgrim, through the wilderness of life. Still my inner storms. Awaken my awareness to my temptations to self-interest and passivity and set my feet on the path to abundant life for myself and this Good Earth. In Jesus' Name. Amen.

Day Four
Now is the Day of Salvation

> *Now after John was arrested, Jesus came to Galilee proclaiming the good news of God and saying, "The time is fulfilled, and the kingdom of God has come near; repent and believe in the good news."* (Mark 1:14-15)

As you walk the highways and byways with your fellow saunterer Jesus, experience God's realm as near and commit to the spiritual and ethical transformation, described in Mark 1:14-15.

I begin each day and every day with the Psalmist's affirmation: "this is the day that God has made, and I will rejoice and be glad in it!" (Psalm 118:24) There is no better day than today to experience God's blessings and inspiration, and I want to be prepared to be blessed and to bless. The time is fulfilled for whole person healing and the realization of wholeness in the lives of persons and institutions. The Realm of God has come near. Indeed, God's realm is right here, in us and among us. God is inspiring us to faithful discipleship for just such a time as now.

With John the Baptist in prison, the Spirit called Jesus to walk forward and claim his destiny as God's Beloved Child and Messenger of God's Salvation.

Jesus calls to us to "repent and believe the good news." The Greek word for "repent" is *metanoia,* translated "to change your mind" or "be transformed." The Apostle Paul challenges us "be not conformed to this world, but be transformed by the renewing of your mind" (Romans 12:2). Each moment challenges us to transformation. To open to God's future is to stand against the values of our culture and embrace God's way of Shalom. As followers of Jesus, we must walk the talk of God's good news and that means embodying in our daily lives the virtues of hospitality, compassion, justice seeking, and peacemaking in contrast to the ways of the world. Our behavior and politics must be congruent with our beliefs.

Truly this is the day that God has made. God's salvation is here. Healing is on the horizon. A day of joy and fulfillment, in which you can be Jesus' companion in healing the world.

God of Creativity and Justice, help me to believe the good news and turn my life from the ways of death to your way of life. This is the day and time for me to claim God's Realm as my polestar and inspiration. In Jesus' Name. Amen.

Day Five
Living in the Immediate

> *As Jesus passed along the Sea of Galilee, he saw Simon and his brother Andrew casting a net into the sea, for they were fishers. And Jesus said to them, "Follow me, and I will make you fishers of people." And* **immediately** *they left their nets and followed him. As he went a little farther, he saw James son of Zebedee and his brother John, who were in their boat mending the nets.* **Immediately** *he called them, and they left their father Zebedee in the boat with the hired men and followed him.* (Mark 1:6-18)

As you saunter with Jesus, meditate on the word "immediately" that occurs twice in this short passage (Mark 1:16-18)

We live in a generous and spacious universe. Yet, each moment calls us to a decision. On those every day and occasionally dramatic decisions, the future rests for ourselves and our planet. As I reflected on the call of Jesus' first male disciples, I remembered a song of my youth, "I Have Decided to Follow Jesus."

> I have decided to follow Jesus
> I have decided to follow Jesus
> I have decided to follow Jesus
> No turning back, no turning back
>
> Tho' none go with me, I still will follow
> Tho' none go with me, I still will follow
> Tho' none go with me, I still will follow
> No turning back, no turning back

> The world behind me, the cross before me
> The world behind me, the cross before me
> The world behind me, the cross before me
> No turning back, no turning back.[7]

In my childhood evangelical church, we were told that this song from India recounted the faith of a new believer, who suffered martyrdom for choosing Christ over his culture. The call of God comes freely but our response may be costly.

We don't know what led to Jesus' call to these particular fishermen. I suspect they had heard him preach and then spoke privately to him. But now was the moment of decision. Now is the time to choose, and in the immediacy of that moment they said "yes" to an adventure with no guarantees or certainties as to where the path will lead. As Dietrich Bonhoeffer asserts, God's grace is free, but it is never cheap. God's grace calls us to follow the way of the Cross, the path of sacrifice, empathy, hospitality, which may put us at odds with family members or our nation's leaders.

Each moment Jesus calls us. Every moment is an invitation to "follow me." Jesus invites us to the Way of Life and when we follow his Way, living out of our own agency as companions, we will have an adventurous life. Sacrifice will be demanded, but in letting go of the past and our limited agenda, we will be reborn in a world of infinite love and energy and in the immediacy of each moment, we discover who Jesus is and who we truly are. The cross of love we bear will be transformed into a hopeful and glorious future with Jesus as our companion.

Today, "I have decided to follow Jesus." I will look at the world with Jesus' eyes and touch the world with his healing hands. "No turning back." In Jesus' Name. Amen.

---

7   "I Have Decided to Follow Jesus," Simon Marak.

Day Six
Liberating Spirit

> But Jesus rebuked the spirit who possessed him, saying, "Be quiet and come out of him!" And the unclean spirit, convulsing him and crying with a loud voice, came out of him. (Mark 1:25-26)

As you read Mark 1:21-28 on your spiritual saunter, consider the difference between "authority" and "authoritarian" religion, politics, and everyday life.

Jesus had authority, grounded in his vocation, self-awareness, and relationship with God. He did not lord it over people or demand unquestioned loyalty. In contrast to many political and spiritual leaders, Jesus walked the talk and talked the walk. His first response to the persons he met was to pay attention to their deepest needs and inner desires and then respond in healing and transforming ways. Even the demonic spirits – and we don't need to know the origin of the negative power that controlled this man – know who Jesus is and are willing to dialogue with him.

Deep within the troubled man, obscured by the powers that controlled him, there was a spirit seeking healing that called out to Jesus, knowing that only the energy of love can heal illnesses of body, mind, and spirit.

When I was a child, I often heard my mother command, "Get thee behind me, Satan" in response to her depression, low self-esteem, and obsessional thinking. She believed that invoking the words of Jesus to Peter (Matthew 16:23 KJV), she would experience relief from the demons that threatened her ability to function as a mother, wife, and schoolteacher. With God's help, she went to work each day for over twenty years, leaving a legacy of success in the lives of her students.

Jesus is on the move, and when we walk with Jesus, we find relief from the forces that would drag us down. As the hymn says, "Jesus knows our every weakness, take it to the Lord in prayer."[8] When we cry out, Jesus responds just as he did to the spirit of health hidden beneath the demonic spirits. With the authority of Jesus, we can challenge the spirits sickness, injustice, and hatred tormenting persons and institutions and trust that with Jesus by our side, we will use our authority to heal and not to harm, to free and not imprison.

Healing Spirit, set me free of all that possesses me so that I might rise like an eagle, free, creative, loving, and empowered to bring healing and beauty to the world. In Jesus' Name. Amen.

---

8   "What a Friend We Have in Jesus," Joseph Scriven.

Day Seven
Healed for Service

He came and took her by the hand and lifted her up. Then the fever left her, and she began to serve them. (Mark 1:31)

As you walk the pilgrim journey with Mark 1:29-34, reflect on the relationship between healing and service.

While Jesus lived in a patriarchal society, the healing of Peter's mother-in-law is not an invitation to women's work but a call to vocation. In her society, one of the primary roles of the eldest woman of the house was hospitality. To welcome a guest was not a chore but an act of respect and consideration. Welcoming and providing a good meal for her son-in-law's teacher was a great honor. Imagine Peter's mother-in-law's disappointment at her inability to serve Jesus. Jesus reached out to her not just to get a good meal, but to enable her to fulfill her vocation for just such a time as now.

Looking at your life, where do you need healing to fulfill your vocation as God's beloved child. What stands between you and living God's abundant life? Visualize Jesus standing beside you, taking your hand, and then lifting you up so that you can fulfill your vocation and serve your world with love.

In *Wishful Thinking: A Seeker's ABC,* Frederick Buechner notes that our vocation emerges from "the kind of work God usually calls you to is the kind of work (a) that you need to do and (b) that the world needs to have done." He continues, "…the place God calls you to is the place where your deep gladness and the world's deep hunger meet." That night Peter's mother-in-law felt delight as she fulfilled her vocation of serving the hungry healer. Let God take your hand, stand up, and serve the world.

"Precious Lord, take my hand, lead me on, let me stand." Give strength to my weakness and energy to my weariness that I may serve you and the world with the work that only I can do. In fulfilling my vocation, let me feel the joy of service as I sojourn with you one day at a time. In Jesus' Name. Amen.

---

9   "Precious Lord Take My Hand," Thomas Dorsey,

Day Eight
Morning Prayer

> *In the morning, while it was still very dark, he got up and went out to a deserted place, and there he prayed.* (Mark 1:35)

On your daily walk with Jesus, consider the role of daily prayer in charting your journey. Read Mark 1:35-39) to guide your adventures today. What is your prayer style and language? How do you understand the purpose of prayer? Does it make any difference to the world?

I describe Mark 1:21-39 as "twenty-four hours in the life of Jesus." The healer is surely on the move, transforming lives through word, touch, and presence. Immediately he goes from one call to another with virtually no break. Jesus even must perform a healing to get his dinner! Of course, if you are a professional, dinner with your colleagues is also work even if it is intended as time of fellowship.

Jesus' time of morning prayer invites us to consider: How do you begin your day? Do you begin the day, rushing about, without intention or purpose? Or do you start the day with prayer, meditation, and intentionality?

For many years, I have gone to sleep, taking a moment to reflect on the day ahead, and if I'm writing, review a sentence or two, and then commit my tasks, and my sleep to God. I awaken with "This is the day that God has made, and I will rejoice and be glad in it." (Psalm 118:24) Then, I brew my morning coffee and sit down to meditate. I begin my day in stillness and intentionality, knowing that even in my retirement, soon I will be responding joyfully to the demands of marriage, grandparenting, teaching, writing, and preaching.

Jesus was busy. But there was peace in his busyness. His "immediately" was spacious and not hurried. He stopped and was fully present for each interruption. Indeed, as Maxie Dunnam says, interruptions called the Healer to prayer. Unexpected events were not nuisances. They were opportunities to usher in God's realm one encounter at a time. The same applies to us: when we center our lives in prayer even the unexpected and annoying can be an opportunity for hospitality, healing, and harmonizing with God's vision. One act at a time, your whole life can become a prayer, as Thomas Celeno said of Francis of Assisi.

When Jesus finishes his dedicated prayer time, he claims his vocation, "Let us go on to the neighboring towns, so that I may proclaim the message there also; for that was what I came out to do." From stillness emerges direction. Prayer orients Jesus' life and our own, even if the external world or our health condition does not change dramatically. Our Spiritual GPS is refreshed and reoriented to meet the providential encounters of the day.

"Sweet hour of prayer"[10] sustain, guide, refresh, and reorient. In stillness, let me hear your voice and find guidance to make each encounter an opportunity to companion you, O Fellow Pilgrim, in healing the world. In Jesus' Name. Amen.

---

10   "Sweet Hour of Prayer," W.W. Walford.

Day Nine
God Wants to Heal You

> *A man with a skin disease came to him begging him, and kneeling he said to him, "If you are willing, you can make me clean." Moved with pity, Jesus stretched out his hand and touched him and said to him, "I am willing. Be made clean!"* (Mark 1:40-41)

Sauntering with Jesus, as you reflect on Mark 1:40-45, embrace God's willingness to support your healing and success, enabling you to become fully alive and fully active in the healing of the world around you.

Psoriasis or eczema won't kill you, but it can make your life miserable. I know this for a fact! In Jesus' culture, it might even define you as unclean and unable to participate in normal religious and community activities. In some cultures, including our own, disease has moral implications. Remember when many people identified AIDS with God's judgment on what they falsely perceived to be the sinful gay community. Such condemnations suggest that God is out to hurt us and not heal us, and that some diseases place us outside of the circle of God's compassion and care.

Perhaps the unnamed man who sought Jesus' aid anticipated that Jesus would say "no." Like other religious leaders he encountered, he expected that Jesus would either be judgmental or disgusted by his physical condition. Instead, Jesus is moved with pity and compassion. In a world in which empathy is considered weakness, Jesus felt the man's pain and uncertainty and reached out to him. Jesus didn't stand aside. He entered the man's world of misery and alienation. Let me repeat: God is out to help us, not to hurt us. Jesus came that we might have abundant life. (John 10:10) God wants us to be agents of our personal adventures and our well-being contributes to God's joy and the healing of the world. While our behaviors may lead to physical outcomes that are detrimental to our health, Jesus welcomes even those of us whose lifestyles– and that includes many of us who have chronic illnesses – have led to negative health outcomes. For Jesus, "this is the day that God has made," "now is the time of salvation," and from this moment on, our lives can be transformed. The past can be healed and the present and future filled with possibility and hope. God calls and, in our response, we awaken God's healing resources within body, mind, and spirit.

In this "immediate" moment, Jesus addresses all our problems with the affirmation, "I am willing to heal you. Be clean. Be renewed. Be forgiven. Come alive."

Healing God, help me to embrace the love that is waiting for me and the healing that is on the horizon. Help me believe that your vision for me is abundant life. Let me claim the healing that is right in front of me and out of my own healed life, be your agent of healing in the lives of others. In Jesus' Name. Amen.

Day Ten
The Faith of Friends Can Heal the World

> *And when they could not bring him to Jesus because of the crowd, they removed the roof above him, and after having dug through it, they let down the mat on which the paralytic lay. When Jesus saw their faith, he said to the paralytic, "Child, your sins are forgiven."* (Mark 2:4-5)

The words of Mark 2:1-12 invite us to claim our role as agents of faith, whose confidence in God's presence in our lives and the lives of our companions enables us to tear down the obstacles to healing and justice.

"When Jesus saw their faith." Often healing is identified with the designated patient's faith. Yet, just as important is the faith of others in our healing, success, and transformation. In his autobiography, *With Head and Heart,* Howard Thurman tells of the transformative power of the world "gentlemen," invoked by President John Hope in his addresses to young African American college students in the 1920s. In the Jim Crow world of dehumanization, diminishment, and death, being called "gentlemen" was a healing balm to Morehouse College students. Respect transforms our spirits. Affirmation gives us confidence that we can succeed. Forgiveness enables us to begin again.

When has a word transformed your life? When has someone's confidence in you given you confidence in yourself? What words do you need to say to yourself or others to restore their (or your) spirit?

When a friend or relation doesn't have faith, we can believe on their behalf. The friends' faith in Jesus' healing power inspired them to break down every obstacle in their way including a neighbor's roof. They believed and God responded. Their faith awakened the inner healing powers within the man's cells and soul.

Faith creates a thin place where God and the world meet. Faith opens the door to new possibilities for God's presence in our lives and in the world. We can, as God's companions on the walk of life, enable God's vision to become more effective to address problems of body, mind, spirit, and politics.

In the case of the man with paralysis, faith leads to forgiveness. Perhaps, it was his sense of sin and limitation that stood between him and embracing the healing available to him. Perhaps, the burden of the past weighed him down in his cells and souls, rendering him paralyzed and unable to claim his own wholeness. Jesus forgives without any action on the man's part. The Healer pronounces forgiveness, the letting go, the elimination, the overcoming of everything that keeps us from becoming the persons God wants us to be. God's love is not transactional; it is graceful, and God's grace is always prior to our response. God's love abounds: while the form of that love depends on our relationship with God and personal decisions, God's love for you has neither beginning nor end and like a good parent, God loves us regardless of the mistakes we've made.

God is in the business of forgiveness, not the business of sin. While our behaviors can harm us and alienate us from others, when we embrace God's forgiveness the burden of the past is taken off our shoulders and we can begin again. We can make restitution and restoration and commit ourselves to advancing the moral and spiritual arcs of history in our relationships and citizenship.

As you saunter with Jesus, for whom are you a mediator of faith? Who needs your affirmation to move forward in life? Who needs your forgiveness? What areas of your life need to be made whole through God's forgiving presence? Remember, and this cannot be repeated too often in a world in which God is seen as a punisher and not a healer, God is out to heal you, not to hurt you, to support you and not punish you, to cleanse you and not diminish you.

Loving God, help me to be an instrument of faith and healing for the persons in my life. Help me forgive and accept forgiveness so that I might rise like an eagle, run and not be weary, walk and not faint, and share my healing with everyone I meet, friend and foe alike. In Jesus' Name. Amen

Day Eleven
A World without Outsiders

> *As he was walking along, he saw Levi, son of Alphaeus sitting at the tax-collection station, and he said to him, "Follow me." And Levi got up and followed him.* (Mark 2:14)

As you saunter with Mark 2:13-17, consider the persons who are your outsiders and how you might find common ground as God's beloved children.

Jesus was a pioneer in spiritual DEI – diversity, equity, and inclusion. He embraced insiders and outsiders, Jews and foreigners, clean and unclean, and women and men, and offered each a path to salvation, healing, and wholeness. In first century Judea, tax collectors were among the most hated class of people: they were generally economically well-off in a society marked by poverty, and they worked for the Roman oppressors. Set apart by their profession, they were barred from the religious and civic activities of their Jewish neighbors. Moreover, tax collectors were known for their dishonesty: since they purchased their positions from the Roman oppressors, they had to set the prices for tolls to make a reasonable profit, thus profiting from an already economically depressed community. While many were simply trying to make a living, others gouged the public to get the best return on their investment.

When Jesus calls, the Roman agent Levi follows and then invites Jesus to join his friends at a meal. In joining tax collectors and other outsiders for a meal, Jesus violates a social and religious norm, leading the "righteous" moral police to ask, "Why does he eat with tax collectors and sinners?" Jesus' open-spirited table fellowship challenges us to ask, "Who are my tax collectors and sinners? Who is outside my circle of compassion? Who do I condemn for their immorality and evil?"

To many of us, the answer is clear. I am not eager to invite a MAGA Christian to dinner nor would I want to sit across the table from Donald Trump, Bibi Netanyahu, or Vladimir Putin. I am tempted to see them as lost souls, beyond redemption. And, yet Jesus confronts me, as he did the scribes and pharisees, the righteous ones of his time, with the affirmation, "Those who are well have no need of a physician but those who are sick; I have not come to call the righteous but sinners."

Jesus' open circle is a gift to the righteous as well as the sinners. When I am tempted to self-righteousness, I recall a hymn of my childhood, "Standin' in the Need of Prayer."

> Not my brother, not my sister,
> But it's me, O Lord,
> Standin' in the need of prayer.[11]

All of us need God's love to heal the unclean and outcast parts of ourselves. Deep down, we pray for healing. If God's circle includes Donald Trump and the red-hatted MAGA Christian nationalist, then it surely must include me as well!

Jesus welcomes all of us to saunter with him and then pause in gratitude for a refreshment, our favorite beverage and a snack. Jesus' circle of love includes everyone and challenges us to be equally inclusive, encompassing even those whose behaviors and policies we must condemn.

Loving God, whose circle embraces everyone, let me see the holiness of those I challenge and experience your love for those who stand outside my circle of love. Help me to join justice-seeking with compassion for the most powerful as well as the least of these. In Jesus' Name. Amen.

---

11   "Standin' in the Need of Prayer," African American Spiritual."

Day Twelve
Stretch Out Your Hand

> *He looked around at them with anger [for it was the Sabbath]; he was grieved at their hardness of heart and said to the man, "Stretch out your hand." He stretched it out, and his hand was restored. The Pharisees went out and immediately conspired with the Herodians against him, how to destroy him.* (Mark 3:5-6)

As you take a walk with Jesus, contemplating Mark 3:1-6, reflect on God's outreach and your willingness to stretch out your hand to heal yourself and the world around you.

Reach out to Jesus. Jesus wants to heal your cells and soul. Jesus wants to bring wholeness to your vocation and relationships. Every moment, Jesus reaches out through the gift of possibilities, insights, synchronous meetings, and providential events. When we reach out to Jesus, like the man described in Mark 3:1-6, the energy of love will flow from God to us to illuminate, energize, and empower us to abundant life and service to others. God heals in season and out. Every moment is an opportunity for healing, regardless of the limitations of our rituals, dogmas, and rules.

In this story, healing leads to hostility. Jesus fails to follow the rules set up by the religious ritual police and the legalists of his time. No religious fundamentalist, Jesus blatantly challenges the rigidity of the moral and spiritual police, for whom rules and regulations, doctrines and rituals, are more important than the well-being of God's children.

God is the ultimate iconoclast and rule breaker. Guided by his suffering and celebrating love, God honors our rituals and rules and recognizes that, at their best, they give structure and guidance for our lives but transforms and challenges them when they stand in the way of human and non-human healing and justice. Yesterday's rules and mores may have worked fine in the past, and ethical principles provide structure to our lives, but more important is living out our walk with Jesus in the concrete person in front of us.

God is also the ultimate relativist. God's vision of love is addressed to each person and situation personally and concretely and God wants us to do likewise. God's love is intimate and relational not generic and abstract, and God commands us to do likewise in embodying love beyond law and compassion beyond commandment. Despite her adherence to the Ten Commandments, Corrie ten Boom lies to German soldiers to save a Jewish family. Rosa Parks defies the Jim Crow seating laws, and is arrested, to affirm her dignity and the dignity of African Americans as God's beloved children. Environmental activist Greta Thunberg is arrested for defying the Israeli embargo of Gaza. Neighbors provide comfort and passage for undocumented residents, threatened by masked and armed ICE agents' intent on their deportation. And, Jesus, in resistance of strict legalism, heals on the Sabbath. A man is healed, and can now live fully, and yet the religious leaders are inflamed with rage and plot Jesus' murder.

Where are you bound by rules that stand in the way of God's realm on earth as it is in heaven? Where do you need to open your eyes to see the concrete needs of the neighbor, stranger, or family member? Where do you need to be more flexible in dealing with the sinners in your life?

God of Ever-Expanding Love, I stretch out my hand to receive your healing touch. I stretch out my hand to serve my neighbor even if I must defy the mores of my society, and my own previous belief system. I open to be a channel of healing to everyone I meet. In Jesus' Name. Amen

Day Thirteen
A Harvest of Righteousness

> *Other seed fell into the good soil and brought forth grain, growing up and increasing and yielding thirty and sixty and hundred fold.*
> (Mark 4:8)

As you saunter on the Way of Jesus, meditating on the growth of seeds in Mark 4:1-20, consider what enables the seeds of God's inspiration and energy to grow in your life. Delight in the flora and fauna around you. What threatens your spiritual, intellectual, and relational growth?

In Jesus' first recorded parable in Mark's gospel, he compares the Realm of God to our response to seeds of possibility and healing sown in our lives. God is sowing seeds of wholeness and creativity, justice and mercy, in every moment and season of our lives, and in the long haul of our gifts, talents, and vocations. God doesn't discriminate. God sows everywhere and in everyone from a red hat MAGA supporter to a progressive peacemaker.

God's sows and we tend God's seeds in our lives. Grace abounds and touches everyone but there are times we treat giftedness of life carelessly, leaving it rootless. Other times, our gifts are choked by busyness and stress. But, when we choose to be gardeners of God's gifts, our lives flourish and abound in fruit for ourselves and others.

The world lives by the incarnation of God, the philosopher Alfred North Whitehead asserts. We have the freedom to respond to God's gifts in our time and place. When we tend to divine possibilities, our lives flourish and God can do more in our lives than we ask or imagine.

What is essential for our growth is to take good care of the moment-by-moment possibilities and graces we receive. As the hymn says,

> Great is Thy faithfulness!
> Morning by morning new mercies I see:
> All I have needed Thy hand hath provided—
> Great is Thy faithfulness, Lord, unto me! [12]

In the interplay of God's grace and our agency, we have everything we need to succeed, prosper, and serve God, "blessings all ours and ten thousand beside." In gratitude, nurture God's seeds to provide an abundant harvest for you and the Good Earth.

Divine Gardener, thank you for the seeds of possibility and healing you have planted in my life. Give me grace to tend this garden so that my life will be a blessing, filled with joy for myself and love and support for the flourishing of others. In Jesus' Name. Amen.

---

12 "Great is Thy Faithfulness," Thomas O. Chisholm.

Day Fourteen
Small is Bountiful

> *He also said, "With what can we compare the kingdom of God, or what parable will we use for it? It is like a mustard seed, which, when sown upon the ground, is the smallest of all the seeds on earth, yet when it is sown it grows up and becomes the greatest of all shrubs and puts forth large branches, so that the birds of the air can make nests in its shade."* (Mark 4:30-32)

On today's spiritual saunter, if possible, notice all the growing things around you as consider the wisdom of Mark 4:30-32. The world is alive with God's wise energy of love and creativity. Each flower shouts "Hallelujah." Every tree claps its limbs in joy. The grass whispers the many names of God. As Maltbie Babcock chants, "This is my Father's/Mother's world/ All creation sings and around us rings the music of the spheres."

During my junior year in college (1973), E.F. Schumacher published *Small is Beautiful: Economics as if People Mattered,* proposing that the heart of an ecological economics involves focusing on the creativity of persons in community, aiming at the common good for their communities and the planet. Schumacher, no doubt, would also affirm in the spirit of Jesus' parable that small is also bountiful. From small beginnings – a mustard seed, an act of kindness, a word of affirmation, a book placed synchronously in your hand, an apparently chance encounter – truly great things can emerge. Margaret Mead asserted the power of small beginnings, "Never doubt that a small group of thoughtful, committed citizens can change the world; indeed, it's the only thing that ever has." And, of course, Jesus' world changing ministry began with dedicated group of women and men who answered the call, "Follow me," and in all their imperfections, became the catalysts for a world changing message.

The world is changed one small act at a time. This moment holds the future of the planet as well as your own personal future. The tyrants tremble when they witness unexpected acts of kindness and sacrifice for the greater good. The tyrants want to stifle your prayers, songs, and voices, and yet when you act out of love their deathful intentions begin to collapse.

No longer able to attend protests and be arrested for non-violent civil disobedience due to health issues, Dorothy Day averred, "I can still pray." Yes, we can pray and millions of prayers for peace and justice can transform the world.

When young Mother (Saint) Teresa told of her plans to serve the people of India, they judiciously queried, "How much money do you have?" The young nun responded, "Two pennies." To which challenged, "You can't do anything with two pennies." Young Teresa countered, "With two pennies and God, I can do anything." That is God's promise to us, "You can do all things with Christ who strengthens you." (Philippians 4:13, my adaptation) Do something small for Jesus. Dedicate one act at a time to bring love to the lonely, compassion to the outcast, generosity to the vulnerable, protest to the powerful, and trust that God will bring forth great things from small actions.

God of Small Things, help me see the wonder of this moment and the importance of every action. Let me choose life and love one act at a time and share my gifts with you to bring healing to this Good Earth. In Jesus' Name. Amen.

Day Fifteen
Peace in the Storm

> *On that day, when evening had come, he said to them, "Let us go across to the other side." And leaving the crowd behind, they took him with them in the boat, just as he was. Other boats were with him. A great windstorm arose, and the waves beat into the boat, so that the boat was already being swamped. But he was in the stern, asleep on the cushion, and they woke him up and said to him, "Teacher, do you not care that we are perishing?" And waking up, he rebuked the wind and said to the sea, "Be silent! Be still!" Then the wind ceased, and there was a dead calm. He said to them, "Why are you afraid? Have you still no faith?" And they were filled with great fear and said to one another, "Who then is this, that even the wind and the sea obey him?"* (Mark 4:35-41)

As you walk along the paths of life with Jesus, reflecting on Mark 4:35-41, you might ponder the storms in your life and the world that threaten to overwhelm you. We are obviously living through a national storm of chaotic and destructive leadership, climate change is manifest in extreme weather patterns and forest fires, and we face our own quiet storms of uncertainty, anxiety, despair, and temptation. Imagine Jesus in the storm with you, quietly assuring you that you will not drown and by his companionship calming the inner storms you experience.

I imagine two miracles as I ponder the story of the storm at sea. The first miracle, or act of power, occurs when the disciples realize that Jesus is with them in the boat. The waves crash and the winds howl, but with Jesus in the boat with them – and us – we will stay afloat. We are not alone. God is with us and nothing, not even the inner and outer storms of life, can "separate us from the love of God." (Romans 8:38-39)

The second miracle is the stilling of the storm itself. Now, I will make a bold statement. Jesus' miraculous power to still the storm is naturalistic not supernatural in character. Jesus acted within the normal cause and effect relationships to activate the deeper laws of nature. Scientific studies suggest that there is synchronicity between our thoughts and feelings and the world around us. Water crystals respond to our positive or negative attitudes. Prayer and positive affirmations influence the growth of plants. Our attitudes can influence our cells and the progress or remission of disease. I believe that Jesus was so attuned to God's universal presence, incarnate in the human and non-human worlds, that his own energy of love could influence weather patterns. If a butterfly flapping its wings in Pacific Grove, California, can contribute to the formation of a thunderstorm in Potomac, Maryland, then the Fully Alive Jesus can naturalistically calm a storm.

Still, the ultimate message of the stilling of the storm is that God is with you in all the storms of life and that God will never, in life and death, leave you or abandon you. The One Who Loved You into Life companions you in life's storms and will receive you with loving arms at the moment of death. With certainty of God's presence in the storms of life, we can join God in providing life jackets for those at risk in the storms of life.

"Precious Lord, take my hand, lead me on, let me stand," and guide me in the storms of life. Remind me that your love is stronger than the evil intentions of tyrants and the challenges I face. "Through the storm, through the night. Lead me on to the light, Take my hand, precious Lord. Lead me home." In Jesus' Name. Amen.

Day Sixteen
Peace for the Troubled Soul

> *The swineherds came to Jesus and saw the man possessed by demons sitting there, clothed and in his right mind...As he was getting into the boat, the man who had been possessed by demons begged him that he might be with him. But Jesus refused and said to him, "Go home to your own people, and tell them how much the Lord has done for you and what mercy he has shown you."* (Mark 5:15,19-20)

You may need a long walk with Jesus to reflect on Jesus' encounter with the man possessed by demons, recorded in Mark 5:1-20. The story raises more questions than answers and pushes us to look at our own lives: Where are we or our nation possessed by forces beyond our control? What demons threaten to dominate us? How do we free ourselves and our nation from the "demonic" possession that is destroying us?

The scripture notes simply that the man was possessed by demons that rendered him dangerous and uncontrollable to himself and the community. The scripture doesn't aim to present a diagnosis, such as those provided by the *Diagnostic and Statistical Manual of Mental Disorders* (DSM) but states that the man is controlled by forces beyond himself that render his own selfhood null and void. He has no central self around which to orient his experiences and guide his decisions.

Today, we might use the medical language of "dissociative disorder," "multiple personalities," or even "grand mal seizures" to describe the man's condition. Without venturing too far into the paranormal, there is also a possibility that persons and institutions may be overcome by "demonic spirits." The world is much more mysterious than we can imagine. What we deem fantasy may be daily experience in some venues. We can look at the realities of Hitler's Germany, Stalin's Russia, the killing fields of Cambodia, Jim Jones in Guyana, or the mesmerizing of millions of self-proclaimed orthodox Christians in our time by cult-like political leaders and conspiracy theories. Moreover, the word "legion" suggests a political context. "Legion" described a battalion of 4,500 to 5,000 Roman occupying soldiers. We know from the experiences of persons after 9/11 and today's political climate that social upheavals can push persons over the edge in terms of mental well-being. Whatever the source, this man was out of control and had no path to wholeness apart from the power of love.

There is a movement toward health even in the demonic. Even the legendary Satan recognizes their dependence on God, and deep-down desires reconciliation. The demons know Jesus. Indeed, they are more perceptive than the mentally stable citizens of the village. They enter dialogue with Jesus, and Jesus grants their wish to enter the "unclean" swine.

Freed from an evil power greater than himself, the man is "restored and in his right mind." Jesus' compassion and courage restores his selfhood. He is so overwhelmed that he wants to become one of Jesus' inner circle of followers. But Jesus has other plans: go home and be a witness to God's healing love. Live out your life, enjoy healthy relationships, embrace your vocation, get married and start a family. No longer a drama king, the man can delight in the simple pleasures of domestic life.

Our problem may not be a fractured out of control self, but we still need to claim our spiritual, relational, and moral integrity. We need to have a renewed and restored vision, a sense of vocation and selfhood, which weathers the storms of life. We need spiritual strength in our troubled times, when our nation appears to be coming apart by malevolent forces larger than any particular individual. We need inner healing so that we can go about the work of healing the soul of the nation.

Restore us, Great Physician, to our right mind. Clothe us in compassion. Inspire us in service. Challenge us to move from self-interest to world loyalty as your companions in bringing health and healing to the soul of the nation and the planet. In Jesus' Name. Amen.

Day Seventeen
The Energy of Love

> *She had heard about Jesus and came up behind him in the crowd and touched his cloak, for she said, "If I but touch his cloak, I will be made well."* **Immediately** *her flow of blood stopped, and she felt in her body that she was healed of her disease.*
>
> **Immediately** *aware that power had gone forth from him, Jesus turned about in the crowd and said, "Who touched my cloak?"* (Mark 5:27-30)

On today's sojourn, reflect on where you need to reach out for healing in companionship with the woman with the flow of blood's story (Mark 5:25:34).

For twelve years, this unnamed woman had been yearning for a healing. We don't know her age. She might have been in her mid-twenties or later in life. Her flow of blood put her on the sidelines of society and religion. She may not even have been able to marry. She had sought the best medical care in her community but saw no improvement.

When she heard the healer was passing through her village, she decided to try one more time. In her heart, she realized that this might be her moment for wholeness. Indeed, the last opportunity for her to experience healing and wholeness. Despite her fear, and alienation from her community, she took a chance, broke the rules of proper behavior, moving through the bustling crowd and then touching the healer. And then, all heaven breaks loose. She feels an energy flow from the healer to her, transforming her cells and her soul. Something has changed. She knows that she has been healed.

Today, many of us live with chronic illness. Even cancer has become a chronic illness as many people live for years with incurable cancer, going from one treatment to another, and constantly poring over disease markers. Chronic illness is burdensome and can separate us from our peers and restrict us, in certain cases, from once familiar activities. Still, we seek wholeness, a remission of symptoms, and a return to ordinary life.

As she walked toward Jesus, the woman was filled with hope. "If I only touch his garment, I will be healed," she repeats over and over again. Until that fateful moment. "Your faith has made you well," Jesus proclaims. But it is more than her faith that heals her. By her faith-filled touch, she taps into the energy of love that brought forth the universe, spins the galaxies, and gives birth to every creature. God's energy – the energy of love, *ki, chi, prana, ruach* – flows everywhere and when we truly connect with that ubiquitous and holy energy, miracles occur. Not violations of the laws of nature, or supernatural intrusions into our world, but life-changing quantum leaps of God's creative and healing power.

Her faith has made her whole. Our faith can transform our cells and give us new energy. Our faith can also enable us to respond with grace and courage to illness and limitation that persists. In the final analysis, beyond the cure, there is a healing, a sense of God's presence, regardless of the outcome of medical treatments or healing touch. This is the peace that passes understanding that comes from knowing that in life and death, we belong to God, and God will never abandon us.

Grant me, O Healing God, the faith that moves mountains and heals cells and organs. Grant me the faith that persists in prayer and protest, even when the results are uncertain. Let me trust my future to you, knowing that in life and death, you are my Companion and Friend. In Jesus' Name. Amen.

Day Eighteen
Give Her Something to Eat

> *And the neighbors laughed at him. Then he put them all outside and took the child's father and mother and those who were with him and went in where the child was. Taking her by the hand, he said to her, "Talitha koum," which means, "Little girl, get up!"* (Mark 5:40-41)

Open to the healing wisdom of Mark 5:21-24, 35-43 as you take a spiritual saunter with Jesus today.

As a parent who faced a child's diagnosis of cancer, I know the desperation that Jairus felt. A leader of the synagogue, and representative of religious orthodoxy, Jairus likely had doubts about Jesus' orthodoxy. Still, as a parent, you will do anything to get a healing for your child, even seeking out the help of a countercultural spiritual teacher, like Jesus. Orthodox theology no longer matters when your child is near death and only a renegade teacher can help. Jairus reaches out to Jesus, and the healer immediately changes plans.

When they arrive at Jairus' house, they are confronted by a crowd of mourners, who advise, "Don't bother the healer. Your little girl is dead." Jesus, however, has a deeper vision. He believes that Jairus' daughter can be restored to life, whether she is dead or in a coma. The crowd laughs at what they deem Jesus' wishful thinking, eliciting an interesting response from the healer. He throws the naysayers out of the house and only lets his close disciples and the parents come to the girl's bedside.

When you are in trouble, and cannot save yourself by your own efforts, you need to gather a healing team. People who believe that you can succeed and respond to the crisis that confronts you. The power of affirmative faith – your own and your friends' – creates a healing circle that magnifies the healing arc of divine love.

Deep unto deep, eliciting the unconscious powers of healing within her, Jesus speaks to the young girl, on the verge of womanhood and awakens her spirit. Then, he tells the parents to get her something to eat. Freed from the limitations of neighbors' negativity and awakened to abundant life, she needs nourishment for the adventures ahead.

When I read this story in seminars and bible studies, I ask the class, "If Jesus just woke you from a deep coma, what would you want him to cook for you?" The answers I receive reflect my students' favorite foods: crab cakes, fried chicken, a good steak, Mama's pasta, turkey with all the trimmings. You see, healing is all about a meal! All about celebrating life and love and delighting in the good things of God's culinary creation! Healing is about joy and bringing joy to others.

What would you like Jesus to cook for you? How would you celebrate your healing?

Today, two decades after my son's cancer diagnosis, he is healthy, successful, and the parent of two teenagers, who now visit our home regularly and like locusts, clear our refrigerator each time they visit! Healing is about abundant life. God wants to serve and sacrifice. God also wants us to enjoy, and commit ourselves to a world in which every child can delight in their favorite meal in the companionship with loved ones.

Thank you, Jesus, for good food and loving companionship. Let me delight in the pleasures of life and out of my delight, work for a world where every family can celebrate and feast on the bounty of your world in safety and love. In Jesus' Name. Amen

Day Nineteen
When God Can't

> *Then Jesus said to them, "Prophets are not without honor, except in their hometown and among their own kin and in their own house." And he could do no deed of power there, except that he laid his hands on a few sick people and cured them. And he was amazed at their unbelief.* (Mark 6:4-6)

Consider the relationship between divine power and human agency, described in Mark 6:1-6 as you take walk with Jesus today.

When Jesus returns to his hometown, he is met with doubt and disbelief. While doubt may have a positive value in preventing us from succumbing to political prevarications, conspiracy theories, and religious cults, inflexible doubt and disbelief can minimize God's ability to transform our lives and communities. God's power is relational and loving. God does not unilaterally coerce the world but works with the world to bring about the highest good in any given situation.

Medical researchers talk about both the "faith factor," the placebo effect, and the "unfaith factor" (my language), the nocebo effect, in health and illness. The faith factor energizes our cells and souls. Conversely, disbelief and negativity can stunt the immune system and make persons more susceptible to serious illness.

God seeks abundant life for everyone and in every situation. The author of revelation describes the essence of God's call and humankind's response: "Listen! I am standing at the door, knocking; if you hear my voice and open the door, I will come in and eat with you, and you with me." (Revelation 3:20) When we open the door in faith, God can "accomplish far more than we can ask or imagine" to transform our soul and cells. (Ephesians 3:20) In Nazareth, Jesus' neighbors closed the door on divine healing and transformation. Yet, despite their unbelief, God's truth goes marching on. Love wins. Jesus never gives up, despite our faithlessness. Even when we turn away, Jesus keeps knocking at the door and whispering to our spirit, beckoning us to say "yes" to his abundant life. As hard hearted as his hometown neighbors were, they could not entirely stifle Jesus' healing power. Jesus still could heal a few sick people. God never gives up on us or our loved ones, and while God can't defy our heartedness, even our heartedness can't prevent God from loving us. Where might you be barring the door or resisting God's aim at abundance in your life? How might you open the door to divine wisdom and energy?

Ask questions. Seek answers. Share your doubts. Be open to alternative explanations. Yet, stay open to God's healing and loving presence, and when you hear Jesus knocking, open the door of your heart and mind and let him in!

Persistent Companion, be with me in my questions and doubts. Let challenges open me to possibilities. When I hear your knock, let me open the doors of my heart, head, and hands to embrace your gracious healing power and share that power with others. In Jesus' Name. Amen.

Day Twenty
A Center in the Cyclone

The apostles gathered around Jesus and told him all that they had done and taught. He said to them, "Come away to a deserted place all by yourselves and rest a while." For many were coming and going, and they had no leisure even to eat. And they went away in the boat to a deserted place by themselves. Now many saw them going and recognized them, and they hurried there on foot from all the towns and arrived ahead of them (Mark 6:30-33)

We need Miller Time for Ministers and Sabbath Time for Seekers. Saunterers, Flaneurs, and Flaneuses are just a step away from a spiritual sabbath. In apparent aimlessness, there is wisdom and intentionality. In the ambient gaze and aimless step, the universe reveals itself in all its wonder and beauty. Wherever we step is holy ground, a place of revelation, a thin place where the Infinite and Intimate meet in their embrace of all creatures great and small. Saunter with an ambient spirit as you reflect on Mark 6:30-33.

Spiritual success led to stress among Jesus' first disciples. They had so many visitors that "they had no leisure even to eat." Sounds familiar, doesn't it? How many of us eat our lunch while checking our email, scrolling social media, or responding to calls and texts. How many of us are so busy that we don't stop to gaze at the color purple or listen to the praise songs of morning birds.

Jesus takes his followers to a deserted place to rest and reflect. For a few hours, Jesus flows aimlessly like the Tao refreshing and renewing himself and his followers. To our surprise, aimlessness gives birth to energy and intentionality. Doing nothing is the prelude to doing everything with grace and compassion.

Do you have a sacred spot in your home, neighborhood, or a sacred path you walk? If not, ask for guidance for finding the thin place of revelation and rest. Each day take time to go to a deserted place to rest, restore, and renew, and from that rest you will flow with God's Tao and then as go with the Flow, "you shall renew your strength; you shall mount up with wings like eagles; you shall run and not be weary; and you shall walk and not faint" (Isaiah 40:31, my adaptation).

God of storm and stillness, calm my spirit, awaken my senses, and inspire me to seek you in silence and find you in action. In Jesus' Name.

Day Twenty-One
A Social Safety Net

> *Taking the five loaves and the two fish, he looked up to heaven and blessed and broke the loaves and gave them to his disciples to set before the people, and he divided the two fish among them all. And all ate and were filled* (Mark 6:40-42)

Ponder the many undeserved blessings of God as you saunter with Mark 6:34-43. God is out to love us, not to hurt us, is a refrain from Jesus' ministry. God loves us before we have achieved anything and God loves us even when we have gone astray, harming ourselves and others. God gives us spiritual and physical nourishment without considering whether or not we deserve it. Jesus says, if people are hungry, feed them, no questions asked. What would the world be like if "all ate and were filled."

When Jesus saw the crowd waiting for him, he had compassion on them. He freely gave them spiritual and theological nurture and then, when he saw that they were faint from hunger, he fed them. At first glance, five loaves and two fish can't feed anyone. But, when we put faith and compassion ahead of pragmatism and judgment, the loaves and fish are multiplied.

Jesus saw the world through the eyes of abundance rather than scarcity. His mission was based on sharing God's bounty. "I came that they might have life and have it abundantly." (John 10:10) This applies to everyone, citizen and stranger, rich and poor, ICE agent and undocumented resident. No one is excluded from God's social safety net or from God's realm of loving companionship. Everyone receives what they need to experience God's abundant life.

God's grace abounds and challenges us to be graceful. When we look at the world through the eyes of scarcity, whether we are privileged individuals or politicians, God says, "Take another look. There is enough for all if we share." The divine safety net says to Elon Musk as well as refugees looking for asylum:

> *Hear, everyone who thirsts;*
> *come to the waters;*
> *and you who have no money,*
> *come, buy and eat!*
> *Come, buy wine and milk*
> *without money and without price.* (Isaiah 55:1)

Even if you don't deserve it, you receive it, no questions asked, and no minimum requirements, even for greedy moguls. As Mahatma Gandhi asserts, "the world has enough for everyone's need, but not enough for everyone's greed." Let us be channels of blessing and agents of generosity, who challenge our leaders to move from self-interest to world loyalty and nation first to planetary compassion.

God of All Peoples, enlarge my spirit. Out of the gratitude for the blessings I've received, let me bless the world. Challenge my scarcity thinking and fill me with an abundant vision and hands to serve and a heart to love. In Jesus' Name. Amen.

Day Twenty-Two
Meditation and Movement

> *Immediately he made his disciples get into the boat and go on ahead to the other side, to Bethsaida, while he dismissed the crowd. After saying farewell to them, he went up on the mountain to pray.* (Mark 6:45-46)

Take a quiet moment with Jesus as you reflect on the rhythm of prayer and productivity and calm and activity. Mark 6:45-52

The feeding of the five thousand is bookended by accounts of Jesus' prayer life. There is a rhythm of prayer and practice that enlivens our spiritual lives and gives healthy structure to our service. Throughout his ministry, Jesus takes time to pray. To align himself with God's vision and feel God's energy flowing in and through him. When Jesus says, "the Father and I are one," (John 10:30) he is speaking both theologically and spiritually. He is uniquely connected with God in his very being and in his spirit. His unity with God is vocational and spiritual.

We share in our unique ways in that same unity with God. As the Artist of the Universe, the Omnipresent God touches each of our lives. Each moment bears divine imprint and thus we can say with the Quakers that "there is something of God" in everyone. We unite with God's Spirit, speaking in "sighs too deep for words" (Romans 8:26), even when we are unaware of it. A commitment to prayer brings God's presence to the surface of our lives, awakens us to God's guidance, and assures us that God is in and with us in all our adventures.

So, take time to pray. Indeed, the busier you are, the more time you should devote to prayer. Interruptions and activities are calls to prayer and immersing yourself in prayer unites your spirit with God's Spirit in creative activity. Thomas of Celano said that Francis of Assisi's life was a living prayer. May the same be said for us. Let each step bring us closer to God and our neighbor.

But the story doesn't end there! After the quiet of prayer, Mark describes a most curious encounter in which the disciples see Jesus walking on the stormy sea and confuse him with a ghost. This account bounds on the fantastic so take time to let your imagination run wild.

The upshot of this ghostly encounter is that recognizing their fear, Jesus climbs into the boat with them, assuring them that a storm cannot harm them. "Take courage. It is I. Don't be afraid." And once more the sea is calm. Jesus invites them to take solace in the promise of his presence. No storm can shake our confidence when we remember that God is with us. We can feel afraid, and we can take our fears to God in prayer and find courage in the struggle.

Loving God, teach me to pray always and everywhere. Let my life be a prayer as I experience my unity with you and all creation. Out of that prayer, let me serve with joy and abundance. In Jesus' Name. Amen.

Day Twenty-Three
The Fringe of Jesus' Coat

And wherever he went, into villages or cities or farms, they laid the sick in the marketplaces and begged him that they might touch even the fringe of his cloak, and all who touched it were healed. (Mark 6:56)

Grateful for every breath and step you take, pray for guidance in terms of where you need God's healing touch. Where do you need to touch the fringe of Jesus' cloak as you ponder Mark 6:53-56?

The quest for healing is universal. Hope for wholeness is also universal. Mark's Jesus is the healer par excellence. Virtually every encounter in the first ten chapters of Mark involves a healing of mind, body, spirit, or relationships. Jesus even offers theological and spiritual healing to those whose images of God have led to self-righteousness or shame. There is a balm in Gilead and to desperate people the healer from Nazareth was the last chance for wholeness.

Jesus is unique in that he heals in a variety of ways: word, touch, energy, forgiveness, hospitality, affirmation, exorcism, and companionship. For Jesus, there is a path to healing and wholeness appropriate to each person in every health condition and season of life. While we are one the spirit, each of us is uniquely "standin' in the need of prayer." God wants to heal us, even when a cure cannot be found and we must live with chronic or incurable illness. Even here, we can experience the Peace that passes understanding, knowing that forever we are in God's hands and that nothing can separate us from the love of God.

God has a personal relationship with each of us, and all of us. As the North African Saint Augustine says, "God loves each of us as if there is only one of us." We don't need our neighbor's healing, nor should we judge our neighbor's needs. We need the healing addressed personally to us with our name on it. God's center is everywhere. God's center is right where you are in all of your unique beauty and pain. The Great Physician knows what you need and presents healing energies and spiritual possibilities appropriate to every season of life and every problem you face.

Where do you need God's presence most today? Where do you need the touch of the Healer's hand? The invitation is clear, "ask, seek, knock," and you will receive a healing, whether you receive a cure. (Matthew 7:7) Even in the valley of the shadow, we need not fear, "for God's rod and staff comfort us." (Psalm 23;4)

Healing God, I bring my whole self to you and ask for your healing touch in my life today. I bring my need for _____ and ask that your love surround and envelope me, that your energy of love fill me, and that your peace calms and empowers me so that out of the blessings I receive, I will bless others. In Jesus' Name. Amen.

Day Twenty-Four
Ever-Expanding Grace

> *He said to her, "Let the children be fed first, for it is not fair to take the children's food and throw it to the dogs." But she answered him, "Sir, even the dogs under the table eat the children's crumbs." Then he said to her, "For saying that, you may go—the demon has left your daughter." And when she went home, she found the child lying on the bed and the demon gone.* (Mark 7:28-30)

You may want to walk a few more steps to deal with the challenges of this passage (Mark 7:24-30) in which Jesus seems to be all too human and suffering from compassion fatigue. You may also reflect on the challenges of race, gender, and ethnicity in our polarized and divided world. How do we honor our traditions and also expand our care to embrace humankind in all its wondrous diversity?

You must wonder why this passage was included in Mark's Gospel. The all compassionate and hospitable Jesus seems to be caught up in the stereotypical and exclusivist thinking characteristic of his peers. He treats an obviously needy woman with what appears to be contempt. Yet Jesus backs down and reclaims his compassion when she challenges his apparent Jewish exceptionalism.

We cannot rule out the possibility that this woman's faith expanded Jesus' consciousness. Her chutzpah astounded him and challenged his brusqueness and apparent racism. When she protested that even the dogs (the foreigners) get the crumbs from the table, Jesus responded, "for saying that [for pushing back and challenging me], you may go – the demon has left your daughter."

An alternative approach to the passage is to see the encounter of Jesus and the Syrophoenician woman as a living parable. Initially Jesus mimics the racism of the chosen people and gets the assent of the dinner guests to his race-based behavior and then pulls the rug out from them by affirming the desperate mother and healing her daughter!

Regardless of our interpretation of this encounter, the healing of the Syrophoenician's daughter introduces the possibility of non-local healing or healing at a distance. Jesus' words radiate across the neighborhood without the limitations of space and time. In a similar fashion, scientists have explored the possibility that prayer is non-local in nature. We can influence the lives of people thousands of miles away, creating a space in which God's quest for healing can be more effective. Once again, Mark invites us to claim our vocation as God's healing partners. As Teresa of Avila asserts, God wants us to be God's hands, feet, and voice – and also God's prayers and vision - without exception in our troubled and broken world.

God of Unlimited Love, help me to love without reservations, to embrace without limitations, and heal without exceptions. In Jesus' Name. Amen.

Day Twenty-Five
Taking Your Medicine in a Prayerful Way

>*Jesus took him aside in private, away from the crowd, and put his fingers into his ears, and he spat and touched his tongue. Then looking up to heaven, he sighed and said to him, "Ephphatha," that is, "Be opened." And his ears were opened, his tongue was released, and he spoke plainly.* (Mark 7:33-35)

As you saunter with Jesus, reflecting on the healing story from Mark 7:31-37, consider the relationship of spirituality and medicine, and ways you can take medicine in a prayerful manner.

For the past four decades, I have explored the relationship of spirituality and medicine and thirty years ago I was one of the first persons to teach a course on spirituality at a medical school. I believe in the power of prayer to heal bodies, minds, and spirits. As my colleague Dr. Dale Matthews asserts "prayer and Prozac." I would add meditation and medication and contemplation and chemotherapy.

In the ancient world, saliva was considered a curative agent. Recently medical research has demonstrated the role of saliva in skin and oral wound healing in vitro and in overall oral health.[13] Jesus gets intimate in this healing, putting his fingers in the man's ears and applying saliva to his tongue. While we may not choose to imitate Jesus' healing modality, we can share God's energy of love through healing touch. Moreover, we can take our medications in a prayerful way. As one who takes daily medications for hypertension, I give

---

13   Human saliva stimulates skin and oral wound healing in vitro - PMC Secret Healing Powers of Saliva (https://pmc.ncbi.nlm.nih.gov/articles/PMC6593997/)

thanks as I swallow my pills and commit myself to more fully caring for my health. All our actions can be prayerful, especially those that promote the well-being of ourselves and others. Wherever truth and healing are present, God is its source.

Loving God, help me to remember that my body is the temple of the Holy Spirit. Let me treat it with respect and compassion. Let me commit myself to my own physical, mental, emotional, and spiritual well-being and seek that same well-being in my relationships and in my citizenship. In Jesus' Name. Amen.

Day Twenty-Six
Corporate Compassion

> *In those days when there was again a great crowd without anything to eat, he called his disciples and said to them, "I have compassion for the crowd because they have been with me now for three days and have nothing to eat. If I send them away hungry to their homes, they will faint on the way—and some of them have come from a great distance."* (Mark 8:1-3)

Consider Mark's vision of abundant compassion (Mark 8:1-10) as you take a walk with Jesus.

When people are hungry whether in Gaza, South Sudan, or Appalachia, only one response is possible for followers of Jesus, regardless of the political or military situation, and that is "Feed them!"

Three days the crowd listened to Jesus' message and experienced his healing touch. Many were so focused on attending to Jesus' words that they forgot to eat or ran out of the supplies they brought with them. As he paused from his message, Jesus was filled with compassion and compassion inspired action. At first, feeding four thousand seems an impossibility with only seven loaves and two small fish. Yet, when Jesus blesses their scant resources, they are multiplied a thousandfold.

Mark never explains the mechanics of multiplication. Perhaps it is a quantum leap of divine energy, the energy of the big bang manifest in just such a time as now. Perhaps upon seeing the contrast of their meager supplies and Jesus' great faith, prudent members of the crowd surprise themselves and pull out their satchels and share what they initially brought for themselves. In any case, we are dealing with a miracle, a revelation of the deeper laws of nature and the deeper movements of the human heart. The miracle reflects God's ubiquitous providential presence and not some supernatural intrusion in a meaningless world.

Compassion multiplies. Greed subtracts. God's world is infinite in energy and possibly. Whereas scarcity thinking is zero-sum in nature: when you gain, I lose; and when humans act, they usurp divine initiative. Faith imagines an ever-expanding world of relationships. When I gain responsibly, you gain as well. When we use our agency for the well-being of others, God has more power to transform the world, and the moral and spiritual arcs move forward, even to the point of making unexpected resources possible to respond to human need.

Martin Luther King asserted that in the graceful interdependence of life, "I cannot be what I am intended to be until you are what you are intended to be, and you cannot be what you are intended to be until I am what I am intended to be." We cannot be fully alive until our neighbors, strangers, and even "enemies," receive the basic ingredients for "life, liberty, and the pursuit of happiness" for themselves and their families.

The future belongs to the empathetic and compassionate. While some idolize the survival of the fittest and glorify the rugged individual, evolution moves forward as much from cooperation as competition. The inspiration for the evolutionary adventure is God's challenge to move from self-interested survivalism to world-affirming partnership. Let us commit ourselves to feeding the hungry, housing the homeless, and healing the sick without regard to citizenship, nationality, sexual orientation, or achievement. This is the Word of God made flesh and dwelling among us.

Heart of the universe, expand my compassion and deepen my empathy. Let my heart grow to embrace all creation as kin, inspiring my generosity and feeding in return my spirit. In Jesus' Name. Amen.

Day Twenty-Seven
Gradual Healing

> *They came to Bethsaida. Some people brought a blind man to him and begged him to touch him. He took the blind man by the hand and led him out of the village, and when he had put saliva on his eyes and laid his hands on him, he asked him, "Can you see anything?" And the man looked up and said, "I can see people, but they look like trees, walking." Then Jesus laid his hands on his eyes again, and he looked intently, and his sight was restored, and he saw everything clearly. Then he sent him away to his home, saying, "Do not even go into the village."* (Mark 8:22-26)

As you walk along with Jesus and Mark 8:22-26 as your companions, bathe your eyes in the beauty around you, whether you are on the seashore, a wooded path, your neighborhood, or a city street. Give thanks for the gift of sight and sense. Rejoice in your ability to experience the wonders of this Good Earth.

Once more Jesus applies an ordinary medical remedy in a healing way. This time however, there is no immediate cure. The man's sight is restored gradually from hazy and indistinct to clear and sharp. Jesus must go back a second time to cure the man's eyesight.

Not all healing, whether emotional, spiritual, or physical, is immediate. Grief is a process and not an event. Childhood trauma surfaces and recedes, and over years we experience a sense of peace even though the memories never fully go away. The healing of a broken bone or a broken heart takes time, and we need to go easy until our strength of body, mind, and spirit returns. The pronouncement of remission and then cure of cancer occurs after months of treatment and observation, and you still return every six months to note any reoccurrence.

In the context of Jesus' immediate healings, we aren't given any reason for this gradual healing. We do notice that Jesus persists in the healing process. He doesn't blame himself or the man for his limited success, reminding us that healing takes time and that at times the healing involves rising above, or feeling peace and claiming agency, despite chronic or ultimately uncurable disease. God's aim is always toward healing. God works continually through our cells and souls, in the world of cause and effect, to bring about the healthiest outcome. We can find God's presence in dramatic moments of transformation, gradual improvement, and in facing what cannot be cured. When there can't be a cure, there can always be a healing, a sense that God is with us, God's love endures forever, and that with God as our companion we have the resources to face whatever lies ahead. Whether we live or die, we belong to God and God has not lost anyone yet, nor will God lose anyone in the future.

God of the growing edge, of mustard seeds and redwood trees, help me be patient with the healing process. Help me recognize that healing takes many forms and that I have a role in the healing processes of life. Bless me so that I may be a blessing. In Jesus' Name. Amen.

Day Twenty-Eight
Who is Jesus?

> *Jesus asked his disciples, "Who do people say that I am?" And they answered him, "John the Baptist; and others, Elijah; and still others, one of the prophets." He asked them, "But who do you say that I am?" Peter answered him, "You are the Messiah."* (Mark 8:27-29)

Imagine Jesus walking beside you, as described in Mark 8:27-30, and asking you, "Who do you say that I am?" What role does Jesus play in your life? How can we best get to know Jesus and his vision for our lives?

It is more important that Jesus has a personal relationship with you than you have one with Jesus! That Jesus loves you more than you love him, though opening to Jesus opens us to powerful energies of healing, transformation and service. Still, Jesus always comes to us personally in the events of our lives, our social location, nation's politics, and personal joys and challenges.

In questioning his followers, Jesus begins with the abstract and objective, "who do people say that I am?" and then asks the truly important question, a matter of spiritual life and death, "who do you say that I am?" Peter boldly says, "You are the Messiah." He is not making a creedal statement or repeating the traditions of his people – although both are true – he is making a personal, existential statement. Jesus is the One he's been waiting for. In his relationship with Jesus, Peter will find meaning and purpose, and hope as he faces his own imperfections and mortality. In Jesus, he will find a way to respond to the troubled times in which he lives – poverty, classism, military occupation, and oppression. In walking with Jesus, he will find his way through the valley of the shadow of death, manifest in the violence of Rome and in his own personal failings. In our quest for a personal relationship with Jesus in our time, I want to repeat the wisdom of Albert Schweitzer:

> He comes to us as One unknown, without a name, as of old, by the lakeside, He came to those men who knew Him not. He speaks to us the same words: "Follow thou me!" and sets us to the tasks which He has to fulfill for our time. He commands. And to those who obey Him, whether they be wise or simple, He will reveal himself in the toils, the conflicts, the sufferings which they shall pass through in His fellowship, and, as an ineffable mystery, they shall learn in their own experience Who He is.

As a child, I accepted Jesus as my "personal savior." Although the contours of my faith have changed radically since that revival meeting in 1961 in King City, California, I have reclaimed Jesus as my "personal savior," and I reclaim him every day. My relationship with Jesus has pushed me from personal salvation and the binary understanding of heaven and hell into the realms of world loyalty and universal salvation far beyond the transactional salvation of my childhood. My personal relationship with Jesus is not about my individual salvation but about healing the world. When I confess that "he walks with me and he talks with me and tells me I am his own,"[14] it is not just Jesus and me in our solitary intimacy, it is Jesus and me companioning in healing the soul of the nation, confronting institutional and governmental sponsored racism and violence in our own nation, celebrating the diversity of humankind, praying and acting for peace in Ukraine and the Middle East, and seeking to share beauty and love as a husband, father, grandfather, professor, pastor, and friend. These are the tasks which Jesus has to fulfill in our time with me as his companion. To know Jesus is to have a larger world with greater empathy and willingness to learn from and serve others.

---

14   "In the Garden," C. Austin Miles.

Who is Jesus for you? In what ways is he coming to you? He is One of Us, the companion of each of us, coming to us in the way we need to find joy and live fully and responsibly in our world.

Thank you for being my companion, Jesus. Thank you for walking beside me, guiding, challenging, and protecting me. I accept you as my Messiah and embrace the task you have for me today. In Jesus' Name. Amen.

Day Twenty-Nine
God Feels Our Pain

> *Then he began to teach them that the Son of Man must undergo great suffering...He called the crowd with his disciples and said to them, "If any wish to come after me, let them deny themselves and take up their cross and follow me. Those who want to save their life will lose it, and those who lose their life for my sake, and for the sake of the gospel will save it. For what will it profit them to gain the whole world and forfeit their life?* (Mark 8:31, 34-36)

As you saunter with the Savior, pondering Mark 8:31-9:1, where do you see great suffering in our world? What is your calling in relation to the pain of the world?

Early Christian theologians split over the relationship of Jesus and God in terms of whether God experienced Jesus' suffering on the Cross. To many theologians, it was impossible for the Eternal and Powerful God to experience suffering. Suffering compromised divine perfection. To others, and I am one of them, suffering and joy, empathy toward all creation, is a witness to divine perfection. While even the most empathetic among us must, for our self-protection, partially anesthetize ourselves to the world's suffering, only letting a portion of the pain and tears into our experience, God is the fellow sufferer who understands, as the philosopher Alfred North Whitehead asserts. Only a suffering God can save, as Dietrich Bonhoeffer rejoins. Only a God who fully embraces the pain and joy of the world, our pain and joy, can heal us.

I grew up singing "What a friend we have in Jesus, all our sins and griefs to bear, what a privilege to carry everything to God in prayer

That means that Jesus' personal relationship with us embraces us our lives in their totality, joy and sorrow, love and hate, hopelessness and helplessness, anger and activism.

God feels our pain. God feels our hopelessness and anger in our feelings of powerlessness to respond to the evils perpetrated by our nation's leaders. God feels from the inside the utter terror of a child in Gaza and an undocumented parent traumatized by ICE in Southern California. God feels from the inside the insecurity and envy of a national leader and his desire to destroy the legacy of his predecessor in the White House to make him look better and erase the gains in human rights in our nation to promote the interests of the powerful and privileged of his race.

Jesus is the Great Empath. He feels and he responds. He is with us at the memorial service and at the wedding. He rejoices at a youth's three pointer on the basketball court and another youth's imaginative inventions. Jesus the Great Empath is our "childhood's pattern," as the Christmas carol proclaims, and we become like him as we grow in empathy and care and seek to ease the pain and expand the joy of the world.[15]

Empathetic Savior, awaken me to the pain of the world, and guide me in bringing healing to the world in my personal relationships and politics. Let me seek the justice that heals and reconciles our Good Earth so that your realm be realized "on earth as it is in heaven." In Jesus' Name. Amen.

---

15 "Once in Royal David's City," Cecil Francis Alexander.

Day Thirty
On the Mountaintop

> *Six days later, Jesus took with him Peter and James and John and led them up a high mountain apart, by themselves. And he was transfigured before them, and his clothes became dazzling bright, such as no one on earth could brighten them. And there appeared to them Elijah with Moses, who were talking with Jesus. Then Peter said to Jesus, "Rabbi, it is good for us to be here; let us set up three tents: one for you, one for Moses, and one for Elijah."* (Mark 9:2-8)

Ponder your mountain top experiences as you climb the mountain, described in Mark 9:2-8, with Jesus as your companion.

We all need a vision of the mountain top. We all need moments in which the world is illuminated, and, with William Blake, we see everything as it truly is – Infinite! The disciples went to the mountain to pray and in that moment had a collective mystical experience. The light that created the universe, the light bursting forth from the Big Bang, enveloped them. All things were connected by love, and the prophets came alive before them. For a moment, controversy was forgotten and fear overcome. They wanted to stay high on the mountain top forever.

Like other mountain top mystics, Peter exclaims, "Let us set up three tents, and dwell with the prophets and you forever." He wants to savor the vision, but God calls him to be both heavenly minded and earthly good. The mountaintop is high only because the valley is low. The heights call us to the depths and mysticism drives us to mission.

On the night before his assassination, Martin Luther King spoke to a crowd of supporters in Memphis, Tennessee: "Well, I don't know what will happen now. We've got some difficult days ahead. But it doesn't matter to me now. Because I've been to the mountaintop. And I don't mind. Like anybody, I would like to live a long life. Longevity has its place. But I'm not concerned about that now. I just want to do God's will. And He's allowed me to go up to the mountain. And I've looked over. And I've seen the promised land. I may not get there with you. But I want you to know tonight, that we, as a people, will get to the promised land. And I'm happy tonight. I'm not worried about anything. I'm not fearing any man. Mine eyes have seen the glory of the coming of the Lord."

Let us seek the mountaintop. Let us aspire to be mystics and to immerse ourselves in God's presence. Let us seek to "dwell in the house of God forever," knowing that God's house is everywhere and God's call for us is to bring the mountain top to the darkest valley and carry our moments elation to a world of pain as mediators of God's vision of Shalom and Wholeness.

Take us to the mountain top, O God, and then guide us to the valley that we may bring the light of transfiguration to the dimness of despair and destruction, transfiguring hate into love and fear into courage to heal the soul of the nation and the planet.

Day Thirty-One
In the Valley of Chaos, God is With Us

> *Someone from the crowd answered him, "Teacher, I brought you my son; he has a spirit that makes him unable to speak, and whenever it seizes him, it dashes him down, and he foams and grinds his teeth and becomes rigid, and I asked your disciples to cast it out, but they could not do so.. It has often cast him into the fire and into the water, to destroy him; but if you are able to do anything, help us! Have compassion on us!" Jesus said to him, "If you are able! All things can be done for the one who believes." Immediately the father of the child cried out, "I believe; help my unbelief!"* (Mark 9:17-18, 22-24)

Wrestle with the words and images of Mark 9:14-29 as you journey with Jesus. How do you bring the illumination of the mountain top to the valley of chaos?

Plato's Myth of the Cave describes the journey upward from the cave of the shadows to the illumination of the sun. Most people, according to the philosopher, dwell in the realm of shadows, mistaking falsehood for truth. By the interplay of divine providence and human agency, a few members of society are compelled to leave the cave and experience the brightness of divine sunlight. At first, they are confused and stumble in the light as if it is darkness. Then, they become accustomed to the light of Truth, seeing reality for it truly is - divine, eternal, and beautiful. Yet, the sight of divine truth drives us to return to the cave to seek to awaken those who dwell in the shadows of half-truths and lies.

From the mountain top of Transfiguration, Jesus and his followers must descend to the world of chaos, sickness, and oppression where they are met by a distraught father, and his demon possessed son. Having failed to secure his son's freedom from the demonic, the father reaches out to Jesus with all his anxiety and doubt, eliciting Jesus' declaration. "I have compassion, and I am able to heal your son."

Like the father in this gospel story, "I believe; help my unbelief" is our mantra. We want to trust God's goodness. We want to lean on the everlasting arms in times of trial. We want to believe that God is on our side and will heal our bodies, spirits, and the soul of the nation. In all our uncertainty, the desire to believe is sufficient to awaken the healing energies within us and those for whom we intercede. God wants you to live abundantly and lovingly.

Like the mustard seed, just a little belief transforms the world. Like the sinking Peter of another gospel story (Matthew 14:28-32), turning our gaze to Jesus enables us to rise and navigate the storms of life. Trusting God, even in our doubt, gives us courage to walk on in the storm, knowing we'll never walk alone. Faith no greater than a mustard seed enables us to face the mountains in our path and realize that God makes a way when we see no way forward.

God of the Mountain Top, help me to bring your love and light to the valley of shadow. Multiply my feeble faith that I might confront the mountains of racism, hatred, xenophobia, and violence and that I might experience your power in my own anxiety and distress. Let me bring light and love to the shadows and calm to the frenzied chaos in my heart and the world. In Jesus' Name. Amen.

Day Thirty-Two
Greatness in Service

> *But they were silent, for on the way they had argued with one another about who was the greatest. He sat down, called the twelve, and said to them, "Whoever wants to be first must be last of all and servant of all." Then he took a little child and put it among them, and taking it in his arms he said to them, "Whoever welcomes one such child in my name welcomes me, and whoever welcomes me welcomes not me but the one who sent me."* (Mark 9:34-37)

In a world of pretenders and prevaricators, consider the nature of true greatness as you walk with Jesus, meditating on the scene from Mark 9:33-37.

While many people prize power, privilege, and possession as their ultimate concern, Jesus defines greatness in terms of service and sacrifice. Those who would be great must be willing to let others succeed and to step aside and let others have their place in the sun. Greatness involves caring for the most vulnerable and powerless, and seeing our solidarity with them. As Jesus says in Matthew 25, as you have done unto the least of these – the hungry, thirsty, and imprisoned – you have done unto me. In the first century, women, children, and foreigners were at the bottom of the social, economic, and religious ladder, and despite their power Romans were considered unclean spiritual inferiors. For Jesus, they are on the top steps and are uniquely loved by God. In being loved, they are invited to transform their values and lifestyle.

This is not transactional salvation and leadership. Our greatness is not concerned with reward. It may even involve sacrifice and getting out of the way so others can get ahead of us. Our quest for greatness is found in humility and service without thought of return. Spiritual stature takes us from self-preoccupation to world loyalty, from concern for the individual self to care for the planet. To see your well-being connected with the well-being of the least, the lost, the laboring, the forgotten, and persecuted. Let me grow in soul so that I can embrace all creation in true greatness and empathy of spirit and see other's successes in the quest for abundant life and justice as important as my own power and privilege.

Parent of all, help me understand that true greatness is found in service and sacrifice, and that abundance and joy are found in empathy and partnership. In Jesus' Name. Amen.

Day Thirty-Three
Many Paths, Many Healers

> *John said to him, "Teacher, we saw someone casting out demons in your name, and we tried to stop him because he was not following us." But Jesus said, "Do not stop him, for no one who does a deed of power in my name will be able soon afterward to speak evil of me. Whoever is not against us is for us. For truly I tell you, whoever gives you a cup of water to drink because you bear the name of Christ will by no means lose the reward.* (Mark 9:38-41)

As you saunter along, noting your current health condition and giving thanks for your health, regardless of your current condition, where have you found healing outside of the Christian community? What non-Christian practices have deepened your faith and well-being? Consider the wisdom of Mark 9:38-41.

In many ways, Jesus was the parent of the contemporary movement of multiple or hybrid spiritualities and holistic medicine. Jesus believed that God's healing was ubiquitous and multi-faceted. God's healing touch is not limited to a particular modality or religious tradition. Like the Logos theologians of the early church, Jesus believed that wherever healing and truth are present, God is its source, even beyond his own religion and culture.

The disciples congratulate themselves on silencing the practitioner of an alternative healing approach. They assume Jesus approves and are stunned by Jesus' affirmation of other healers. God is not stingy in terms of revelation and healing. We can experience God everywhere and, in all things, and God uses a variety of practices and medications to promote well-being. Today, Jesus would be described as a holistic healer, who honored Western technological medicine (after all, he used saliva!) and also utilized the placebos (faith), touch, energy, affirmations, and words to heal.

As followers of Jesus, let us be open to a variety of tested and helpful techniques. Let us do all that we can to promote healing through our personal generosity and through advocating for health care, healthful diets, and safe housing for everyone, not just in North America but across the globe.

Healing God, inspire me to seek my well-being and the well-being of others. May your healing energy flow in and through me to bring wholeness to my cells and soul and add to the health of those around me and across the planet. In Jesus' Name. Amen.

Day Thirty-Four
Blessing the Children

> *People were bringing children to him in order that he might touch them, and the disciples spoke sternly to them. But when Jesus saw this, he was indignant and said to them, "Let the children come to me; do not stop them, for it is to such as these that the kingdom of God belongs. Truly I tell you, whoever does not receive the kingdom of God as a little child will never enter it." And he took them up in his arms, laid his hands on them, and blessed them.* (Mark 10:13-16)

Take Mark 10:13-16 on a walk with Jesus. Consider the children in your life and awaken the child in you. Do something playful on your saunter! Skip, dance, sing!

Each month, our congregation sponsors a Messy Church service, aimed at bringing the generations of our congregation together for art, song, scripture, play, artwork, and supper. We all know that children can be messy and noisy, and sometimes adults become annoyed when children laugh or play in church.[16] While there are times for quiet, there is also time for celebration, laughter, and movement.

Mark notes Jesus' annoyance at the "worship police," who discouraged children from seeking his blessing. To the dismay of his followers, Jesus took the children in his arms and blessed them.

Every child needs a blessing. Every child needs to be told that they are loved and that they matter.

Today's children need a blessing. Many are too anxious and too busy with after-school activities. Others don't have enough to eat. Some

---

[16] For more on Messy Church, see Home - Messy Church USA (https://messychurchusa.org/)

are neglected due to parents working two jobs to make ends meet. Still others are starving in war torn lands like Gaza and South Sudan.

Jesus blessed the children, and he wants us to bless them too. He wants us to spend time with the children in our lives, to listen and play with them, to let your love be incarnate in words and hugs. He wants us to advocate for food, shelter, health care, and safety for children, and for welcome at our churches. Jesus doesn't recognize national borders, nor does Jesus want our solemnity to prevent children from delighting in being part of our congregation's life. He simply says, "bless the children," and create a society and planet where every child can flourish.

Bless the children! Feed the children! House the children! Welcome the children! For they are the realm of God in our lives.

Loving God, bless the child in me and in those around me. Let me welcome every child with love. Let me advocate for tangible blessings of supportive adults, safety, nutrition, housing, education, health care, and security for every child. From my blessings, let me bless others. In Jesus' Name. Amen.

Day Thirty-Five
Wealth that Lasts

> *Jesus, looking at him, loved him and said, "You lack one thing; go, sell what you own, and give the money to the poor, and you will have treasure in heaven; then come, follow me." When he heard this, he was shocked and went away grieving, for he had many possessions. Then Jesus looked around and said to his disciples, "How hard it will be for those who have wealth to enter the kingdom of God!"* (Mark 10: 21-33)

Take Jesus on a walk in which you discuss the interplay of wealth and poverty in North America and in your immediate community. Reflect on your own material attachments as you read Mark 10:17-31. What stands between you and God's Realm being realized in your life?

Several years ago, an investment company asked potential customers, "Will you outlive your money?" This is an important question to semi-retired and retired senior adults like me, which asks us to reflect on what is truly important in life beyond our financial assets. In his encounter on the road with Jesus, the rich young man rightly affirms his moral integrity and faithfulness to the Jewish law. Yet, he is unable to do the one thing needful to become a committed member of God's Realm, divest himself of his fortune. His attachment to wealth, despite his goodness, is the one thing that stands between him and the fullness of God's Realm.

Mark 10:21-33 is one of the most countercultural scriptures in the New Testament. It certainly goes against free market capitalism and consumerism. "How hard will it be for those who have wealth to enter God's Realm?" Wealth insulates and isolates. In the twenty-first century, wealth – even inherited wealth – is seen as a sign of God's favor and hard work. In tax policy, not to mention economic legislation, the wealthy don't have to justify their wealth or how they use it, while the poor must justify their poverty. While people like me might on occasion spend $200 for dinner with companions, we criticize the poor for purchasing a pizza, buying a bottle of wine, or cable television, forgetting that everyone deserves a celebration.

Jesus' Realm turns everything upside down. Those consumed by wealth are in dire threat of losing their souls by placing their privilege ahead of their loyalty to God and care for the vulnerable in their midst.

The theologian Paul Tillich once asked, "What is your ultimate concern?" and noted that your ultimate concern, your priority, has a godlike function in determining what is important to you, what you are willing to live for and die for. Our ultimate concern promises complete fulfillment and demands complete sacrifice.

In this encounter, while Jesus is not opposing having sufficient resources to buy a home, car, and go on holiday, he is asserting that extreme wealth gets in the way of our relationship with God and our neighbor. In his time and ours, the reality of great wealth while people are starving goes against the values of God's Realm. The wealthiest – and even those like me who are comfortable in retirement – do not "deserve" to hold onto our wealth while others scramble from day to day. We must consider the "least of these" in our economic decisions, household expenditures, and tax policy. We must seek to live more simply so that others may simply live. Such values are obviously un-American in our society that rewards wealth and punishes poverty and praises consumerism while avoiding sacrifice. Yet, at the end of the day, the only values that matter are spiritual, embodied in our relationship to God and one another. Seek God's Realm and you will have everything you need!

Wake me up, God of all creation, to the cries of the poor and my complicity in their poverty. Grant me a generous spirit and a heart in solidarity with the vulnerable and poor. In Jesus' Name. Amen.

Day Thirty-Six
The Way of the Cross

> *"Look, we are going up to Jerusalem, and the Son of Man will be handed over to the chief priests and the scribes, and they will condemn him to death; then they will hand him over to the gentiles; they will mock him and spit upon him and flog him and kill him, and after three days he will rise again."* (Mark 10:33-34)

As you saunter with Mark 10:32-34, imagine how the disciples responded to Jesus' foreshadowing of his death and resurrection. How do you respond to the image of a God who feels your pain and suffers with you?

The sacrificial spirit of Philippians 2:5-11 permeates Mark's Gospel. Christ is the model for our own decision-making and value system.

> *Let the same mind be in you that was in Christ Jesus,*
> *who, though he existed in the form of God,*
>   *did not regard equality with God*
>   *as something to be grasped,*
> *but emptied himself,*
>   *taking the form of a slave,*
>   *assuming human likeness.*
> *And being found in appearance as a human,*
>   *he humbled himself*
>   *and became obedient to the point of death—*
>   *even death on a cross.* (Philippians 2:5-8)

The way of the Cross is the way of life, according to Dietrich Bonhoeffer. The German theologian, who was executed for resisting the destructive and diabolical Nazi regime, believed that only a suffering God can save, and in saving us through humility, Jesus is the pattern for our own lives. To follow Jesus is to make decisions that often go against our self-interest, whether they involve economics, privilege, and power. To follow Jesus is to live sacrificially and in service of the human community and planet.

We don't know in advance the path of our personal Way of the Cross, the sacrifices we must make to be faithful to Jesus' Way. We nevertheless need to be ready to let go of our comforts and power to follow Jesus' Way of healing service. The cost may seem greater than we can take, but the way of the Cross leads home and those who lose their lives for God's way will gain their souls and experience companionship with God in all the joys and challenges of life.

Help me, Suffering God, to take up my cross of caring for the world in daily acts of kindness, service, and sacrifice. Let your mind guide my mind on life's narrow pathway and let me find joy in the journey toward justice and compassion. In Jesus' Name. Amen.

Day Thirty-Seven
Glory that Matters

> *James and John, the sons of Zebedee, came forward to him and said to him, "Teacher, we want you to do for us whatever we ask of you." And he said to them, "What is it you want me to do for you?" And they said to him, "Appoint us to sit, one at your right hand and one at your left, in your glory..."* [to which the reply was] *"...whoever wishes to become great among you must be your servant, and whoever wishes to be first among you must be slave of all. For the Son of Man came not to be served but to serve and to give his life a ransom for many."* (Mark 10:35-37, 44-45)

Reflect on our society's values in contrast to Jesus' values as you take Jesus and Mark 10:35-45 for a walk.

"The Son of Man came not to be served but to serve and to give his life a ransom for many." As the Cross looms on the horizon, Jesus reveals the true nature of divinity embodied in a fully alive human. God does not "lord it over us." God is not like Caesar or Herod, demanding loyalty and punishing enemies. God is not like the wealthy potentate who seeks to amass power and possession. God serves and sacrifices. God becomes one of us, undermining every earthly vision of power.

"Whoever wishes to be great among you must be your servant, and whoever wishes to be first among you must be slave of all." Turning the world on its head, Jesus wants us to let go of the individual self and join with the Self of the Universe. Jesus wants us to exchange self-interest for world loyalty and see our well-being as connected to the well-being of our neighbors and people we will never meet, the child in Gaza or the inner city, the polar bear drowning in the Arctic, the unborn child of generations born in 2025. Jesus calls us to be "mahatmas," great souled persons of stature, who are kin to all creation, for this is what God is – the Heart of the Universe, the force without power, and the only power that matters, the power of healing love.

Open my senses, Heart of the Universe, to your beating heart in all creation. Let me see your face – and my connection – with everyone and call all creation kin. In Jesus' Name. Amen.

Day Thirty-Eight
What Do You Want God to Do for You?

> *Then Jesus said to him, "What do you want me to do for you?" The blind man said to him, "My teacher, let me see again." Jesus said to him, "Go; your faith has made you well." Immediately he regained his sight and followed him on the way.* (Mark 10:51-52)

In a sauntering conversation with Jesus about today's reading (Mark 10:46-52), talk with Jesus about where you need healing.

Sight impaired Bartimaeus saw Jesus' as his last hope for healing. As Jesus saunters past him, greeting an adoring crowd, he shouts at the top of his lungs. He is so disruptive that his neighbors seek to silence him. But, always prepared to change course, Jesus immediately stops and beckons Bartimaeus to his side.

While Bartimaeus' obvious need is the restoration of sight, Jesus nevertheless asks, "What do you want me to do for you?" Sometimes there is deeper need beneath the obvious one, and Jesus wants Bartimaeus to consider what he really wants out of life. "Let me see again!" The answer is physical, and it may also be spiritual, "let me see the world as it is; let me see the world fresh with new eyes; let me see differently discovering divinity in the domestic and holiness in everyday life."

When Jesus asks us "What do you want me to do?" how will we answer? Dig deep and don't hold back. Our response may transform our lives.

God of Questions and Possibilities, challenge me to self-examination. What do I really want out of life and what will I sacrifice to find the healing and change that I need? Open my eyes to the world around me, that I may see clearly, and respond lovingly to your call. In Jesus Name. Amen.

Day Thirty-Nine
The Tale of Two Parades

> *Then they brought the colt to Jesus and threw their cloaks on it, and he sat on Many people spread their cloaks on the road, and others spread leafy branches that they had cut in the fields. Then those who went ahead and those who followed were shouting,*
> *"Hosanna! Blessed is the one who comes in the name of the Lord!*
> *Blessed is the coming kingdom of our ancestor David! Hosanna in the highest heaven!"* (Mark 10:7-10)

Take a jaunty walk as if you are walking into Jerusalem with Jesus. Imagine shouting "Hosanna" with the crowd. Maybe even shout "Hosanna" yourself (Mark 11:1-11).

Theologians and bible scholars Marcus Borg and John Dominic Crossan suggest that there were two parades on that first Palm Sunday. During Passover, the population of Jerusalem doubled to 400,000, a time of celebration but also potential threat to Roman occupation. At one of the gates of the city, Jesus entered riding on a colt, a donkey, a symbol of peace, greeted by palms and praises, and no swords or spears. On the other side of the city, Pilate entered: desiring to make a show of force to tamp down any threat of revolt, the governor was accompanied by "cavalry on horses, foot soldiers, leather armor, helmets, weapons, banners, golden eagles mounted on poles, sun glinting on metal and gold," as Marcus Borg and John Dominic Crossan note.

What will we choose – the Way of Peace or the Way of Domination? The Power of Love or the Love of Power? Tragically, followers of Jesus then and now have succumbed to the way of power, putting Caesar before Jesus, doctrine before love, orthodoxy before hospitality, and uniformity before adventure. Philosopher Alfred North Whitehead, the philosophical parent of process theology, describes the tragedy of Western Christianity in his magisterial text *Process and Reality*:

> When the Western world accepted Christianity, Caesar conquered…The brief Galilean vision of humility flickered throughout the ages, uncertainly… But the deeper idolatry, of the fashioning of God in the image of the Egyptian, Persian, and Roman imperial rulers was retained. The Church gave unto God the attributes which belonged exclusively to Caesar.

There is an alternative Way of Life, the Way of Jesus on Palm Sunday, resisting evil through peaceful affirmation, challenging injustice through prophetic healing. Even as he turns over the tables of injustice and greed in the Jerusalem Temple, Jesus is charting another way: a World in which everyone is encircled by love, welcomed at the table of abundance, and affirmed in all their wondrous diversity. Have the mind of Jesus, the apostle Paul says, in Philippians 2:5-11. Let go of individualistic power and domination, control and superiority, and join the sacrificial Jesus in saving the world through compassion and kindness.

Hosanna! Loud Hosanna! Don't let your Hosanna be half-hearted! Praise God who brings beauty and justice to this Good Earth and join Jesus in the parade!

Let me, God of Praise and Service, sing Hosanna and shout for joy as I march with Jesus in the Way of Shalom. In Jesus' Name. Amen.

Day Forty
Who Will Roll Away the Stone for Us?

> *When the Sabbath was over, Mary Magdalene and Mary the mother of James and Salome bought spices, so that they might go and anoint him. And very early on the first day of the week, when the sun had risen, they went to the tomb. They had been saying to one another, "Who will roll away the stone for us from the entrance to the tomb?"* (Mark 16:1-3)

Nothing is more moving than a resurrection, especially in the wake of the deathful reality of the Cross. Out of the inertness of death springs forth resurrection life. Consider the stones standing in the way of serving God and reaching your full humanity, as you read Mark 16:1-3. How will they be rolled away? What will open a way where you currently perceive no way forward?

The women's anxious question, "Who will roll away the stone for us?" is one of the most desperate pleas in scripture. They have lost everything. Their world has fallen apart. Their beloved teacher and friend, who treated them as God's children and not second-class, has died a horrific death, and a stone stands in the way of their future. Hopeless, they still yearn to present Jesus with one last act of love.

"Who will roll away the stone for us?" presents the concrete obstacles that put our future hopes in doubt. The stones stand in the way of the desperate yearning of a mother in South Sudan, Gaza, or Appalachia, seeking to ensure a good diet – even a morsel – for their emaciated child. The despair and helplessness we feel as we view masked and heavily armed police rounding up unarmed and law-abiding undocumented residents and separating children and parents, traumatizing whole communities, and putting our democracy on the brink of destruction. The anger we feel at a Christianity that has abandoned the power of love for the love of power, and chosen Caesar over Jesus and violence over the Sermon on the Mount. The pain of a loving spouse at the graveside, wishing they had a few more years together.

Healing and empowerment emerge in the concrete limitations of life. Within the pain is the possibility for healing and transformation. Within the righteous, anger prophetic healing is born, and a new social order is born.

Gautama Buddha noted that life is suffering, and this suffering comes from our holding on to what must by necessity change. While it is just part of the picture, suffering and despair may drive us to agency and protest and to the embodiment of new spiritual and relational values. The old ways lead to diminishment, destruction, and death. New possibilities, an alternative future, must be imagined as we hope against hope that God will make a way forward where we see no way.

What are the stones in your life? Where do you despair about the future? Where do you ask, "Who will roll away the stone?" or "Can these dry bones live?" God is present in the despair and hopelessness. In the darkest night, a glimmer of light shines and the eye begins to see. God makes a way where there is no way. But we must wait and then join God in pushing the stone out of the way and marching toward the horizon of our dreams and hopes.

Holy One, in the darkness, give me light. In uncertainty, a ray of hope. Companion me as we make a way forward where at first none seemed possible. In Jesus' Name. Amen.

Day Forty-One
An Empty Tomb and an Open Future

> *But he said to them, "Do not be alarmed; you are looking for Jesus of Nazareth, who was crucified. He has been raised; he is not here. Look, there is the place they laid him. But go, tell his disciples and Peter that he is going ahead of you to Galilee; there you will see him, just as he told you." So they went out and fled from the tomb, for terror and amazement had seized them, and they said nothing to anyone, for they were afraid.* (Mark 16:6-8)

As you journey toward God's open future, what does it mean to practice resurrection in 2025? What is it like to have Jesus on the road with you? Where do you imagine your sauntering with Jesus will lead? (Mark 16:1-8)

Resurrection happens when we least expect it. When the path forward is blocked, the stone is rolled away, and we are beckoned toward a starting and wondrous tomorrow.

Most scholars believe that the Gospel of Mark ends at verse 8 and the remaining verses of chapter sixteen are a later addition. Perhaps the original ending was lost. Perhaps, for dramatic purposes Mark completes his gospel with a hint of mystery. Perhaps, the resurrection is intended to leave us breathless and open to whatever amazing future God has in store for us and our communities. We cannot anticipate or control resurrection, we can embrace it and let it empower our journey forward in surprising and countercultural actions to heal the soul of the nation and the planet.

Two thousand years later, the future is uncertain and mysterious. Where will we find the Living Jesus amid the rubble of democracy, the falling bombs and tribal conflicts, the irrationality of political leaders, a dying planet, the result of our own greed and thoughtlessness? We need a resurrection, an empty tomb, and an open future for our nation and planet.

Mandated by the angelic messenger to share the good news and bear the Great Commission, the women are overwhelmed. Awestruck and amazed, they say nothing. But eventually, they find their voice and share the wondrous news that Jesus is alive. The grave cannot hold him. His Spirit is released into the world, unhindered and unpredictable, and breathing new life in the dry bones of our spirits.

Regardless of how we understand the ending of Mark's Gospel, the empty tomb gives birth to an open future. Agnostic, unable to describe the resurrection, we simply must awaken to its presence in the uncertainties of our own life. In his poem, "Manifesto: The Mad Farmer's Liberation Front," farmer, environmentalist, theologian, Wendell Berry urges, "practice resurrection." Be as unpredictable and countercultural, as mysterious and resistant as the Risen Jesus. Jesus is alive and we can agents of resurrection in our world. As the apostle Paul stated some twenty years before Mark's resurrection was penned, "Do not be conformed to this world, but be transformed by the renewing of your minds, so that you may discern what is the will of God - what is good and acceptable and perfect." (Romans 12:2)

Resurrection defies logic and upends the machinations of those who want to control the course of the human adventure. Resurrection puts an end to deathful living, despite its apparent victories on the battlefield and in the White House. Resurrection is the ultimate resistance, the resistance defying death in all its forms, physical, emotional, spiritual, relational, institutional, and political.

Jewish mysticism, as articulated by Isaac Luria, uses the term "zimzum" (*tzimtzum*) to describe God's contracting of divine power and energy so that the world could be created and humans discover their own creativity. God makes space for our agency and companionship in healing the world. Perhaps this is at the heart of Mark's mysterious resurrection. We don't receive a clear description or inflexible doctrine.

The resurrection stories are meant to unfold in companionship with the Sauntering Savior. We are left with an empty tomb in defiance of death and an open future beckoning us to become agents and activists of resurrection in our time.

Behold! The Risen Jesus is everywhere. You will meet him sauntering on a residential street, hiking in the wilderness, marching in the nation's capital, and flaneuring on an urban avenue. He comes to us disguised in adventure and possibility and as we saunter, with a vision but an open calendar, we will discover who Jesus is and our own destiny along the Way.

Filled with resurrection hope and energy, we chant the –

We are marching in the light of God,
We are marching in the light of God,
We are marching in the light of God,
We are marching in the light of God.
We are marching…oooo…
We are marching in the light of God.[17]

God of Resurrecting Love, help us to practice resurrection. To be agents of new life. To resist evil by initiating good. To defy death by our liveliness. Let us see you on the Way, follow, and create paths of our own, sauntering with Jesus. In Jesus' Name. Amen.

---

17   "We Are Marching in the Light of God," South African Song.

www.ingramcontent.com/pod-product-compliance
Lightning Source LLC
LaVergne TN
LVHW041633070426
835507LV00008B/590